Brother Marcus Muhammad and Sister Cecelia Muhammad

Have you just about given up looking for Mr. Right or Ms. Right?

1. Does it seem that all the "good men" and "Good women" are taken? ___ Yes ___ No

2. Are you frustrated going to the Church or Mosque, health clubs and just about everywhere else hoping to connect with Mr. Right or Ms. Right? ___ Yes ___ No

3. Are you about to settle for Mr. Ho Hum or Ms. Ho Hum because you cannot find them in your town? ___ Yes ___ No

4. Are you continually disappointed with men and women because they just don't measure up to your Dad or your Mother? ___ Yes ___ No

5. Are you still going to the same places doing the same things with the same people and never meeting the man or woman you are looking for? ___ Yes ___ No

6. Are you waiting for God to mysteriously deliver your future husband to you without you having to do anything? ___ Yes ___ No

7. Do you think living with someone is a practical way to prepare for a strong marriage? ___ Yes ___ No

8. Do you think that once you are married your real life will finally begin? ___ Yes ___ No

9. Do you find yourself believing that he is "the one" every time you start to date someone? ___ Yes ___ No

10. Do you find yourself in abusive relationships but always believe this one will be different? ___ Yes ___ No

If you've answered any of these questions "Yes," then I urge you to read this book, and begin taking steps toward the relationship *you've always hoped for.*

Marriage really is a beautiful thing and the more you think about it you learn to appreciate what marriage could be. The words you say to each other at your wedding will be words of unconditional commitment. No one ever says, **"I am committing to you for the moment ... but, let me be very clear, I make no promises that this marriage will last."** Before you say **"I do,"** you must be willing to make sure you do whatever it takes to make the marriage last for keeps. Your level of commitment is the most vital factor in determining the success or failure of your relationship. Marriage is one of God's greatest and most life-changing ideas. There is nothing like it. Still, healthy marriages do not appear out of thin air, as a wish granted by the marriage genie. But with intentional preparation and hard work, you can build the strong foundation that you'll need to make your marriage last a lifetime.

Marriage gets a bad rap because most people are really bad at it. It's not marriage's fault. It's the couples' fault for being neither mature enough nor smart enough to manage. Committing your heart to someone is a huge decision. If you choose poorly, you could suffer years of heartache or wind up abused or divorced. However, if you select a marriage partner wisely, you could enjoy a lifetime together of intimate love and passion.

Sadly, some couples rush toward marriage as soon as they taste the initial burst of romance. They may have only courted for a few months, but their blissful feelings convince them that they are destined for each other. By contrast, other couples date for years but never find the courage to make a commitment. They so dread marrying the wrong person that they do not marry at all. In the midst of these extremes, how can a single adult sensibly decide whom to marry?

We used to believe people couldn't possibly promise to love someone else in 10, 20 years when neither their partners nor they will be the same people they are now. But that's the point. We know that the future is filled with uncertainty.

Regardless, we still want that promise because it gives us courage to give ourselves to another without reservations. You may not be able to keep that promise, but you can keep the promise to do your best to be an amazing life partner. That's all anyone can really ask for.

*****

"I love you" is arguably the most beautiful phrase in the English language (or any language, for that matter). The meaning, however, isn't as clear as you might expect. Even poets and authors say that words fail to capture the essence of love. Words just don't do love justice. Love isn't some mythological creature that we hunt to no avail for all of eternity. Love is a state, love is a duty. And it's not just the state of the people in the relationship; it's the state of the relationship itself. Let's look broader. It's the highest, grandest and most coveted of all the states of being. No human in the world isn't looking for love. It's important to ask yourself these three questions before you tell people you love them. Why? Because saying "I love you" is more sacred than sex. It holds much more meaning. Here's what to ask yourself?

What does it feel like for another human being to tell you, "I love you" Depending on how experienced you are with love, you may take the emotions you're feeling to mean more than they actually do. Love isn't just about the emotions you're experiencing. Those emotions are your mind's way of sensing there is potential for love to form. Happiness, excitement, nervousness and maybe even a bit of worry are all signs that the chemistry and connection the two of you share may very well be nurtured into love. While the emotions associated with love are certainly a part of the whole experience, there's much more to love than that. Remember that emotions come in response to our interpretation of our reality, and that interpretation will change over time. If you base your whole definition of love on emotions alone, your relationship is doomed to fail.

Will saying "I love you" benefit the relationship? Sometimes it's too early to say 'I love you.' It just is. Sometimes you say it before you're certain you're in love, and you find yourself wishing you could take it back. Maybe you've said it too soon. Maybe you've scared your partner and ruined what could have been a beautiful thing. You won't always know when the time is right, so you're going to have to go with your gut. Nevertheless, the more information you have about your feelings for each other, the better. If you're going to go with your gut, make it an informed and wise gut. I'm not someone who believes things will just work out if they're "meant to be." I believe you have to be smart to make a relationship work — and sometimes that means waiting to make sure you mean it when you tell your partner "I love you."

Why are we saying it? Why? What's the point? Take a moment and seriously think about this. We don't do things just for the sake of doing them. No matter how uninformed, naïve or plain stupid people can be, our decisions usually have some logic behind them. We do things because we believe doing them will give us the results we want. So, let us ask you again: Why do you want to tell your partner how you feel? Is it just something you want to say? Is it something you just want to "get over with" because you've been stressing over it? Are you saying it because you want to hear your partner say it back? Because you feel like it's a thing you're supposed to do? Is your reason selfish? We think that because loving is supposedly a selfless act (which it, in fact, isn't, but we won't get into that here), telling people we love them is selfless. But are you saying this because you believe it will make your partner happy? Is it something you believe your partner wants to hear? There is really only one perfect moment to tell someone "I love you." It's the moment you feel your love needs to heard. When you tell someone you're in love, it's not just because you love this person. It's because you know that hearing those three words roll of your lips will change your partner's life for the better. That's when saying "I love you" embodies true love.

This is why Pre-engagement counseling is so helpful when you are interested in marrying someone. It is impossible to uncover by yourself every potential problem area of your relationship. Even wise friends and family can overlook negative warning signs. Therefore, seek a trained Pre-Engagement counselor to discuss the details of your relationship before you get engaged. I promise it is well worth it even if you have to go out of your way to find it. The counselor my wife and I chose was perceptive and showed us areas that could cause problems for us in the future. For instance, we discovered that we deal with our free time quite differently. Neither of us was right or wrong; we were just different. Fortunately, the counselor revealed this issue to help us become more sensitive to each other. Rather than fight about our free time, we learned to value what the other person prefers. This is just one example of how pre-engagement counseling improved the harmony of our relationship. The decision to marry someone is so significant; please do not bypass the wisdom of outside counsel before engagement. If you can meet with someone trained to deal with relational problems, you can save yourself a lot of heartache. Furthermore, a good counselor can help save you from marrying the wrong person.

How to Marry the Right Person

It's a commonly asked question: "How do I know if I'm marrying the right person?"

Finding Miss or Mr. Right is not always an easy thing to do. Once you think you have found the right person, you may have **doubts**. Having doubts about who you are marrying is not only normal, but healthy.

Hopefully you already know that **you should not marry someone** who drinks too much, spends too much, works too much, brags too much, uses drugs or other illegal behavior, has been unfaithful, cruel, dishonest or abusive.

If your future spouse is free of those destructive behaviours and you are still having doubts about getting married, read through these statements. You will see if your doubts are reasonable and worth paying attention to or if you are having **cold feet** about getting married without having any rational reasons.

Happiness and Emotional Support

Although expecting a spouse to make you feel happy all the time is unreasonable, being with the right person can bring **happiness** and a sense of personal strength to your life.

5   Ways You Can Tell It Is Love

You will know you are marrying the right person when you feel support and encouragement about your own growth both emotionally and intellectually. The right person will want you to be emotionally healthy and able to stand on your own two feet. When you are with the right person you will feel good about yourself, safe, and fulfilled.

The right person will not be negative, selfish, wishy-washy, silent, embarrassing, critical, or a slob. Why spend your life with a jerk?

Affection, Love, and Sex

It is important that the person you marry is someone who is understanding and agreeable to your wants and needs when it comes to sex and affection.

You will know you are marrying the right person if your future spouse says "I love you" not only in words spoken, but by loving actions. We define loving actions as doing things such as noticing when you are tired, remembering your birthday, wanting to spend time with you, listening to you, showing you respect, calling if you are running late, showing you affection, being patient with you if you don't understand something, kissing you hello and goodbye, and hugging you for no particular reason.

You will know you are marrying the right person if you are sexually compatible with one another. If the two of you view **sexual intimacy** differently or have vastly **different libidos**, your **marriage relationship** will suffer.

The right person is someone who you like and who is your friend. The right person will enjoy spending time with you. Your love and your **marriage** will slowly fade if the two of you are not friends.

The right person is kind, considerate, and polite. Little things in life such as saying 'thank you' and holding a door open may seem old fashioned, but they do reflect the amount of caring and kindness in a person.

Communication, Goals, and Values
You and the right person will have similar goals and values in life.

Having different likes and different opinions is okay as long as the two of you agree to disagree. Although you may not always agree with one another, conversations with the right person will be interesting and not boring. The right person will communicate thoughts and feelings with you and will not keep hurts and concerns bottled up inside.

Understanding that the only constant in life is change, the right person is willing to discuss **marriage issues,** questions, and topics with you both before and after you get married.

The right person will encourage you to make decisions to live a healthy lifestyle by eating healthier foods and getting exercise. The right person will want to work with you to balance your work and personal lives.

Feeling as if you are the only one picking things up around the house or taking care of the children can get old. The right person is willing to share in the responsibilities of your home and future children.

Finding the right person doesn't mean that the two of you won't have difficulties or differences to deal with. However, with the right person you will know that the two of you will be able to work through the issues that could hurt your relationship. You should also believe that your partner would seek professional help if you both were unable to work things through on your own.

Trust and Honesty
The right person is honest with you.

The right person will trust you and not monitor your phone calls, or computer usage, or limit the amount of time you spend with others you care about. You will know you are marrying the right person if your future spouse does not try to isolate you from your family and friends.

Is it good to do things with friends but without spouse?
What will we do if one of us really likes to hang out with so and so and the other doesn't?

You not only need to belong to family, friends, groups, etc., you have the right to do so. The right person in your life will not try to control your life but will want to share a life with you. The wrong person will make you feel as if you have to walk on egg shells in order to keep peace in your home.

You should not have to defend wanting privacy or time alone. You will know you are marrying the right person when you are not questioned about your need for time alone or personal space.

The right person will trust you and not spy on you. Feeling as if you have to justify your every move will become a very heavy burden.

Red Flags in Your Relationship

If you realize that there are red flags or problematic issues in your relationship, don't ignore them or delude yourself into thinking that the red flags aren't that important or that someone you love will change. It does take more than love to have a successful **marriage**.

Take Your Time

Every person and every relationship is different. Slow down and take time to think through these and other issues you may not have considered. Give yourselves the gift of time and the reassurance that you are the right person for this commitment. If the above questions raised concerns or issues that you and your partner haven't discussed or thought about, maybe the relationship needs more time before you say, "I do."

Questions to Ask Yourself

Below are a few thoughts for you and your partner to consider and discuss before committing to marriage. Answer the following questions for yourself, using as much time as necessary to consider each issue fully and making notes of your responses and reactions.

Also, share the exercise with your partner and allow him or her to consider it privately. Afterwards, schedule a time and place to discuss your responses in an environment that is free from distractions and stress.

If you're thinking about tying the knot then be sure that your future life partner to-be can honestly answer these questions to your liking:

Why am I getting married? Why am I choosing to share my life, resources and dreams with this person? What has brought me to this point in my life? Why is this the time? There are many reasons for wanting to find a marriage partner: companionship of a spouse and wanting a family (a spouse and children).

What would marriage give you that you don't already have? What would you be giving up? You can list your pros and cons of marriage. The major issues that come up are about the loss of freedom in marriage. You have to account for the other person in all your decisions. There seem to be more family obligations when you are married. This can take up a lot of your time. Being single can take a lot of time too. One of my clients desires to find a wife so he can focus more of his energies on his business. He figures he spends at least 16 hours a week searching for "the one."

On the other hand, wanting a spouse to support you through life's ups and downs is a big motivation for marriage. Also, having a steady companion for meals and leisure time seems to be high on the list "for" marriage. It is up to you to weigh the pros and the cons and to figure out if the scales tip towards or away from marriage.

How do you view marriage? What's your opinion of marriage? Do you have positive thoughts about marriage? Or do you have a negative view of marriage? My friend Abdullah — early 40s, single and never married — has parents that are divorced. She claims that she knows very few happy marriages. The view that **"most marriages end in divorce"** surely impacts her readiness for marriage. A woman's ex-boyfriend once referred to her as "his ball and chain" to one of his friends. He has never married and is in now his late 40s. Don't you think this perspective on marriage may have prevented him from taking marriage seriously?

How much of your time would you be willing to devote to a life partner? What are your top priorities in your life? List your top priorities in life. If finding a marriage partner or making the most of your current relationship is one of the top two, then you are probably ready for marriage. Another client had a good job that was relatively stable and a good social life of friends. The only thing missing in his life was a marriage partner. He really wanted to settle down and have a family. He was tired of running around to singles events. This became his top priority in his life. He did end up meeting his wife at a dinner at a local meeting.

Are you willing to make the compromises to be a "we" instead of a "me?" Once you find the person you believe to be "the one," are you willing to sacrifice in order to make the relationship work? I have friends who met at a singles weekend. He was from Washington, DC and she was from Boston. The woman moved to DC and found a new job in order to have this relationship work. On the other hand, I had a male friend in New York engaged to a woman in Boston. Neither was willing to move. Needless to say, the marriage never happened.

Are you emotionally available for a relationship? What are the circumstances that make it difficult for you to commit to marriage right now? Have you moved on from your past divorce or most recent break up? Do you have commitments such as your children, an aging parent or the financial strain of changing careers? One of my clients did not feel comfortable courting until her last child moved out the house when she left for college. Are you truly open for courting and a serious relationship that can lead to marriage?

How will you know when you are ready for marriage? Trust in yourself that you will know when you are ready for marriage. When you find that someone special, you just know. There is a synergy and a flow! If you find someone who shares your values and your life goals, you will just click with the other person. We have witnessed this time and time again with both our clients and my friends.

Some people just know that they want to be married, and for others, it takes the right person to come along. Kareem, a man in his mid-30s, told me, **"I never thought about marriage until I met** my wife. I just knew she was the right marriage partner for me."

One thing I've noticed is that those who are ready for marriage are tired of the dating merry-go-round. They want some kind of stability in their life. They desire to spend their energies on building a relationship and want to get beyond the "good for now" mindset.

Are you willing to go public with your desire to find a marriage partner or to be married? Marriage is not a dirty word.

We tell our clients to be very upfront about their intentions to find a partner for marriage. **"Won't I scare the guy away?"** is a question we are often asked. Our answer is, **"If he is scared to talk about wanting to find someone for marriage, then let him be scared away. The right person will stick around because he is interested in the same thing you are."**

One of our male clients from L.A. met a woman online in Philadelphia. She told my client that she just wanted to be friends. He told her that he has plenty of friends and that he is looking for a marriage partner. This man is clearly ready for a marriage. He is willing to stick to his goal. We commend him for his focus and determination.

So, you are the only person who can say if you are ready or not for marriage. It takes giving yourself a very honest assessment. If you ask yourself the above questions, you will get closer to answering the question, **"Am I truly ready for marriage?"**

Do my parents, friends, peers or co-workers support my choice or are they concerned for my welfare? How do I feel about their apprehension? Have I really made a good choice for me or have I compromised my values because I hope things will get better? We encourage you to seek the support of your friends and family. Since these people generally know you well, they can offer helpful insight on whether you and your court ship partner are a good match. In addition, they are not as emotionally blinded as you are and may identify problem areas that you have overlooked. Should someone raise a concern about your relationship, focus on the facts and do not hide the truth. Be willing to admit that you might have neglected a problem. Parents and friends are not always right, but you should consider their legitimate opinions. They may have years of marriage experience to back up their concerns, and ignoring them would be foolish. Listen with an open mind to what they say about your relationship. Remember, however, that the final decision rests solely in your hands. Parents and friends can state their feelings, but don't allow them to decide for you. Instead, let loved ones be resources to aid in your decision-making process.

When you make one of the biggest decisions of your life, having the support of your family and friends is a wonderful blessing. It not only gives you a sense of peace but also assurance that they will be there for you if times get hard. No married couple is an island. You will need the encouragement of others—especially if you have children. You endanger your dating relationship if you hide it from people. Instead, ask yourself if those near to you are excited about your relationship moving forward, and examine why or why not. Don't underestimate the benefit that those close to you can have on your relationship.

Why do you love me?
People seem to feel this is a question that doesn't especially need answering. Most will say we love others simply because we love them — a horrible answer. All people need to know exactly why it is that they love the people they love. Loving someone is a very selfish act, and it's okay. You love the person you love for what that person does for you and how he or she makes you feel. We may all have slightly different answers as to why we love someone, but if we aren't able to exactly define the parameters of our love, then we're likely to struggle later on once the initial intensity dies down. If your partner can't answer why he or she loves you now, then imagine the inevitable uncertainty down the road.

Why do you want to spend the rest of your life with me?
"Because I love you" is not a good answer. Life is a journey — one that is best not traveled entirely alone. However, not everyone has the same destination in mind. Wanting to take different pit stops along the route is one thing. Wanting different things out of life is another entirely. Your partner should be able to tell you what life experiences he or she hopes to share with you. It's these little goals you set for yourselves that make your life special.

Will you do your best to keep the romance alive?
Keeping the romance alive is not an easy task. Yes, it's all mental, but keeping interest for such a long time is difficult. It takes a lot of work and creativity. It takes the other person regularly trying to please and impress you, which in itself becomes increasingly difficult with each new year. Romantic love cannot survive on its own; both of you are going to have to maintain it constantly. Is your partner willing to keep the romance as one of his or her main priorities?

Will you grow with me, and not away from me?
We may not know exactly where our lives will take us and what we will learn — who we will become — along the way, but we can make a conscious effort to grow closer together and not apart. Most people grow apart over the years because they feel like they've accomplished everything in their relationships that needs accomplishing. This is one main reason marriages end up being so horrible — people think that there is no greater peak to climb than the one their relationship is already resting on. Marriage shouldn't be the end, it should be the beginning.

Will you stick through the rough times?
The good times are a piece of cake. The difficult times, however, will destroy your relationship if you allow them to. There comes a point in every relationship when you have to make a decision. It's a decision that, if made, is only made once. You will reach a point where you will either decide you are going to be there

for this person for the rest of his or her life, or not. If you decide you're going to stick with this person then you can't allow any tragedy or outside force to shake that decision. This is one of the most important decisions we make in our lives — or, as it often turns out, fail to make decisively. Has your Court mate made the decision? Have you?

Are you willing to lose some battles in order to keep the peace?
The key to a successful marriage is taming your ego. No matter how competitive we are, sometimes you just need to pick your battles. Sometimes the arguments and the stress just aren't worth it. What you need to understand is that 99 percent of arguments aren't arguments over fact, but rather over opinion. An opinion is neither right nor wrong. Sometimes you just have to let things be.

Can you promise to put us ahead of everything else?
Life has a lot to offer. And if you're anything like me, you have a very large appetite. We want everything life has to offer, and then some. The problem is we don't have enough time to have it all; our lives are too short. We can only pick a few things we consider important and do our best to flourish in those areas. The beauty of marriage is that it can be used as a base to build the rest of your life on. Your partner should be just that: your partner. Your relationship is the most important thing in your life because it's what makes the rest of your life possible.

Will you be a great parent?
Again, how could anyone know he or she will be a great parent? Easy. You just decide you're going to be. That's it. No tricks. No gimmicks. Just a decision and then action. Some things don't need too much thinking involved. You're going to be great because you decided you will be. Will your Court mate do the same and be a great role model for your children?

Will you be sure to remind me how much you love me regularly?
People not only want, but need to hear it. We need to be reminded

you love us because we know that love doesn't always last forever. We want to hear the words and then have that reassurement reinforced with actions showing how much you love us. It really is enough just to love us, but understand you need to love us the way we need to be loved — just like we need to love you the way you need to be loved in order for you to be happy.

Can you promise to do all you can to keep that spark alive?

Sparks don't spark on their own. Think about how a lighter works. You have a spark that lights the fuel, which creates a flame. But how does that spark, spark? You have to create a force that will result in the energy creating a spark. Just the same, you can't expect sparks to keep flying if you're not trying. If you want to have a happy and healthy marriage, then you need to find someone willing to devote the necessary energy.

Will you support me if I can't support myself?

Not just financially, but mentally. Maybe even physically if necessary. No one knows what life holds. The unexpected happens, often leaving us weak, hurt or even permanently damaged. Will your partner carry you when you can't walk? Will your partner support you when you're weak at the knees? Will your partner carry the family you've created until you regain your strength? Is your partner capable of mustering the strength to fight battles for the both of you?

Will you promise to continue to pursue your personal goals and dreams?

Marriage is not entirely the end of the person you were and the start of a new you. Sure, being in a serious relationship does require a person to change in many ways. Yet, there's a part of us we can never, under any circumstance, let go of. The dreams, wants and hopes we have — our personal goals — must stay alive. When we lose them, we lose ourselves and inevitably lose the person we love. Marriage isn't just an "us." It's also a you and him / her. You have to juggle being the person you have always been with being a part of a larger whole. It's not easy. But it is necessary.

Will you not allow yourself to let go?
Will your partner take care of him or herself by eating healthy and exercising? Will your partner get regular checkups and take vitamins? This may sound silly, but we've seen what letting yourself go can do to a marriage. Moreover, I've seen how not maintaining your health can make the lives of those closest to you incredibly difficult. Yes, your family should take care of you when you need to be taken care of — but it's your responsibility first and foremost to take care of yourself. No people should become a burden to those they love.

Do you have, or have you had any, sicknesses or physical problems that could affect our relationship? (Allergies, cancer, eating disorders, venereal disease, etc.)
Do you believe in divine healing, and how would prayer relate to medical attention?
How do you think about exercise and healthy eating?
Do you have any habits that adversely affect health?

If I'm the first to go, will you be there with me until the end?
Will your partner hold your hand when you're too weak to hold it back? Will your partner kiss your forehead and tell you he or she loves you, that you made life worth living? That, because of you, life made sense? Will your partner be there for your last breath, when you find yourself pressed betwixt fear and content? No one should leave this world alone. It's said that we leave it the way we come into it, but even when we come into it, there's someone there to hold us. I understand most people don't like to think about death, but seeing as it's an inevitability, it's better to plan ahead.

Can you promise me that if my time is cut short, you'll continue to live on for the both of us?

You love this person. You want him or her to be happy regardless of whether he or she is with you or without you. If death collects you ahead of schedule, you'll want to know during those last few seconds that the person you love will continue to live life to the fullest. That your partner will continue to do great things, continue to be happy, and — if you have children — continue to love your children and guide them through life. The death of a loved one can ruin you. It can break you in ways that make full-recovery impossible. Can your partner promise you to find the strength and courage to press forward? I don't know about you, but the last thing I'd want for the woman I love is for my departure to be her downfall. If my being in her life or leaving her life will in anyway destroy hers, then I clearly made a mistake by allowing myself into her life.

We've always wondered why couples spend so much time planning for their wedding, but so little time planning for their marriage. The wedding is a fantastic celebration of a couple's love for one another. But it lasts only one day. A marriage, on the other hand, for better or for worse, impacts the rest of your life.

In order to help you think deeply about your future marriage and reduce the statistical wreckage that surrounds marriage in our culture, we've created five crucial questions you should answer and discuss before you say, "I do!" These questions are not easy, but they're essential for thoughtful consideration.

Are You and Your Courtship partner Willing to Work at Premarital Education?

With divorce rates soaring, think about this fact; there is a 31 percent better chance a couple will stay married if they are willing to work at premarital education and counseling. The main reason for an engagement period is to prepare you for marriage, and adequate preparation requires significant work.

It's possible for engagement to be a fun, romantic season of life that you'll treasure forever. But it can be an extremely crazy time, full of many decisions that need to be made, where tensions can run high and some conflict can be expected.

Few couples ever think deeply about it, but the main reason for an engagement period is to prepare you for marriage, and adequate preparation requires significant work. Successful marriages are often the product of healthy premarital decisions and a willingness to work on the relationship before they say "I do."

Here are a few of our recommendations for resources that are available for you to help you prepare for marriage:

Read a book together. No business person would start a new company without putting energy and time into finding out all they can about their new business. Yet couples go years and even a lifetime doing marriage by circumstance and chance. So pick up a book on preparing for marriage and put effort into it.

Find a good premarital counselor or mentor. Proverbs 11:14 states, **"Where there is no counsel, the people fall; but in the multitude of counselors there is safety."** This biblical principle applies to all areas of our lives, but it screams "this makes sense" in the context of getting married. We suggest you meet with someone at least 4 to 6 times before the Big Day.

Talk about everything. Having honest dialog about the key issues you face as an individual and as a couple is critical to moving your relationship forward.

Are You and Your Courtship partner Willing to Hear From Your Relational Community?

These days, many engaged and pre-engaged couples don't love the idea of inviting family and friends to share opinions about their relationship, but we all need friends and family who will be honest about their thoughts, fears and concerns.

It would be wise of you to give permission to those you trust to speak the truth to you. Such people will have your well-being at heart and won't be motivated by their own baggage or ego. What a gift those people can be to you! Seek them out, listen carefully, and then together discuss what you heard.

Relational baggage can develop when someone pursues fulfillment through a person, possession, or substance rather than the love of Almighty God. Baggage can surface in a variety of forms, such as addictions, eating disorders, abortion, debt, or divorce.

Unfortunately, almost everyone carries some type of baggage, so do not assume that your man or woman that you are about to marry is immune. Before you give someone your heart, determine if he or she is wrestling with any baggage issues.

Also, understand that the consequences of certain baggage may never disappear completely. An addiction can keep someone in poor health. A divorced single may regularly have child custody problems. If you want to marry someone who happens to have these kinds of issues, you might face some very tough circumstances when the person's past resurfaces. If you are not prepared to deal realistically with them, the repercussions could easily dominate your relationship. Discuss your concerns with a Counsellor or see your local Dianetics Auditor if you feel unsure about how someone's past might affect you.

Please do not downplay relational baggage—it has the power to destroy your relationship. Sometimes, these complex, negative issues require years to resolve. Do not expect that marriage will make them disappear. You will generally have to wait until a person overrides his or her baggage with the truth of God's love before real healing takes place. Therefore, if your date carries emotional baggage, please vigilantly deal with it before you get engaged. Marrying someone who is free of baggage is worth the extra months or years of waiting.

Are You Willing to Look Honestly at the "Red Flags"?
People who ignore red flags in the relationship, won't discuss them, or even worse, expect them to go away, are headed on a journey toward disaster. No one gets married hoping to be miserable, but too many people who ignore red flags mistakenly assume things will get better when they are married. Marriage only gets more complicated if couples haven't worked through the issues beforehand.
What are some of the red flags you should be willing to look at? Frankly, there are many red flags you would be wise to consider, but here are a few we consider most important:

1) Addictions,
2) A history of being abused or of being an abuser,
3) Unfaithfulness,
4) Warnings from your community,
5) Differences in spiritual values,
6) Poor communication and high conflict.

Are You Willing to be Ruthlessly Honest About Your Own Brokenness?

No one is perfect. Everyone has been hurt. The truth in relationships is that hurt people, hurt people. When it comes to your future marriage, there is really only one person who can make a change, and that is you. Trying to change your partner may seem like a noble pursuit, but trust us; you won't change your fiancé. The best gift you can give your spouse is a commitment to work on your own spiritual, physical, mental and emotional health.

You can, however, change yourself. The best gift you can give your spouse is a commitment to work on your own spiritual, physical, mental and emotional health. You will be ready for marriage not when you have your life in perfect order but rather when you are willing to admit to yourself, your fiancé and to God that you are responsible for your own brokenness. You must be willing to do all you can as an individual to deal with your brokenness in order to bring stability and health into the relationship.

If you're in a committed relationship and have either discussed marriage or can sense you're minutes away from a proposal, congratulations! Now, take a deep breath and ask yourself these crucial questions before you start deciding between princess and sheath bridal gowns. When you find the right person, marriage is absolutely amazing. But it's also work. More work than the actual work you get paid to do. And a big part of the work we have to do when we're married is on ourselves. But many of us fail to realize that some of that work can actually be done before we walk down the aisle. Before you take the plunge, ask yourself these nine questions, which will prepare you for the realities of wedded bliss.

Can I live on my own?

I know, I know, you're about to live with your partner, assuming you don't already, so what's the point of this question, you may be asking yourself. Too many men and women make the mistake of assuming marriage means never having to be alone again. Wrong! A healthy relationship requires that both partners know how to be happy and fulfilled on their own first, before they take on the responsibility of helping to make another person happy. Make sure you're looking to settle down with someone who adds great joy to your life, but who you aren't saddling with the unrealistic task of creating joy in your life.

Do I like my partner just the way they are?
People don't change. I mean, maybe they'll open their minds to some of your vegetarian meals or take up running or yoga during the course of your relationship. But, when it comes to real changes in their personality — it's probably not going to happen. Marry someone for who they are and not for the potential you see.

Do I expect my partner to be my everything?
The answer should always be: NO. Keep your friends and expect him / her to keep their friends. See them as often as possible and don't make a big deal about their desire to do the same. Invite family members over for dinner. Whatever you do, don't use your marriage as an excuse to hide away in Universe You, Population: 2. Your future spouse can't be your confidante, lover, therapist, trainer and sole source of amusement at all times. Branch out and give them and yourself a break.

Can we communicate well?
You may know your partner very well, and vice versa, but if you could read minds, you'd probably be making a fortune down on the boardwalk at Atlantic City. You have to learn how to be honest and direct with your emotions and needs or you're going to be very disappointed when you learn he / she isn't always going to pick up on your extremely subtle nonverbal cues.

Can I rely on my partner when times get tough?
Because times will get tough. Parents and loved ones will pass away. Children will get sick. You will get sick. I don't mean to be a Debbie Downer, but you need to enter marriage feeling pretty darn confident the person you're committing to won't run for the hills the second something goes wrong.

What role will I play in my family's financial health?

Money isn't romantic and too many couples refuse to talk about finances because they stick by the popular attitude: We're getting married for love, not money. Of course you are — but discussions about finances are essential before you commit for life. Pour yourself a glass of apple juice and spend a night hashing out the logistics of how you're going to pay the rent and put bread on the table. If you plan on having children, who will stay home with them? Will you hire a nanny? When you avoid talking about money, you wind up having money problems. And money problems are one of the major reasons couples fight — and divorce. Managing the money is a household chore, who would manage the money, set the budget, reconcile the checking account, prepare tax returns in your marriage? Because one person's debt becomes a shared responsibility in marriage, when do you reveal a substantial liability or obligation? Student Loans? Have you a clear idea of each others financial goals and obligations (loans, family assistance, as well as support agreements)? Do we have compatible ideas about spending and saving, long term (retirement saving) as well as short term (next car, appliance, or home purchase)? This is an important question, many marriages that fail do so because money and finances are one of the biggest conflict areas couples traditionally face. And a lot of that comes down to having enough or not having enough. This is an important question to define.

Do I want children? Does he?

You may have plans to travel for five years and dine at every restaurant in the world before you have children. That doesn't mean you shouldn't know exactly where your partner stands on children. And you have to be honest, as well, and let your future husband / wife know whether you have always dreamed of having three boys and two girls, have no intention of ever having children, only want to adopt or were told as a teen that you couldn't have kids and will have to consider infertility treatments. Other questions about children that should be answered honestly by both parties: Should we have children? If so, when? Why?

How many?
How far apart?
Would we consider adoption?
What are the standards of behavior?
What are the appropriate ways to discipline them? How many strikes before they're . . . whatever?
What are the expectations of time spent with them and when they go to bed?
What signs of affection will you show them?
What about school? Home school? Public school?

If we do have children, will they be raised with faith?
Many interfaith couples go on to have brilliant, strong marriages, but not if they avoid discussing the elephant in the room. Certain religions require or recommend that both partners adhere to the same faith and, in those cases, you're going to have to make some pretty tough decisions about whether one partner is willing and happy to convert. If you plan on having children, it is essential that you sort this out ahead of time because it will obviously affect them most.

Do I know about my partner's health issues? Does he know about mine?
If you have a health issue that you haven't yet discussed, for whatever reason, your partner absolutely has every right to know about it. If you find it difficult to discuss, make an appointment with your doctor and ask your partner to come along with you. Once you get married, you will have a responsibility to care for one another, and you both deserve to know whether your partner needs an extra level of care before you say "I do."

Have we discussed the name question? Will either or both of us change names, will we hyphenate two names? Will we form a new name and how will our children, if any be named?

What is your date's real age?

Women are not the only ones that lie about their age, men do it too. If you are considering someone for a long-term relationship you should know all of their vital statistics including his or her age. Be gentle when asking this question so not to offend.

What is your date's family background and place of origin?

Find out which country your courtship partner is from and where his or her parents were born. Do they still follow the customs of that country? Do those customs and rituals clash with your own? If your courtship partner was born in the same country as you what city is he or she from? Did they grow up in an urban area or a rural atmosphere? Did he or she grow up as an only child or with siblings? Are their parents still married, if not which parent were they raised by? All of these circumstances shape the person that you are considering pursuing a relationship with. Don't commit to a stranger, learn as much as you can about how they grew to become the person that he or she is today.

What is your courtship partner's current job title and where does he or she hope to be in the future?

What a person does for a living can say a lot about who they are. Find out if the lifestyle required by his job meshes with your lifestyle. Does he or she have to work over night shifts? If so how frequently? Is the work that he or she does life threatening or dangerous? Can you handle that level of stress? Does the work that they do require frequent travel? How do you feel about that? Is wealth most important to him or is he more concerned with work / life balance? How do their goals complement or conflict with yours? It's important to know where your date is now and where he or she is headed in the future so you can know if you want to go along for the ride.

How many serious relationships has your Courtship partner had in the past and why did they end?

It is often advised not to bring up past relationships in a courtship with someone new. This advice is only partially correct. Past relationships shouldn't be discussed on the very first date but before you get too emotionally invested you should learn about their past. Has he or she ever been in love before? Why did those previous relationships end? Do they blame all of the failures of the past on the other person or do they take some responsibility? The things they say about past relationships can give you insight into patterns he or she has in interpersonal relationships. Your partner will probably treat you very similarly to how he or she treated past partners. Make sure you gather some information about the past before you decide if you want a future.

What are your Courtship partner's expectations for a future relationship?

You should find out if you and your partner are on the same page as to what you are looking for. How relationship minded are they? Is he or she just looking to play the field or are they ready to settle down? If they say that he or she is just looking for something casual or if they say they are just looking for new friends but doesn't want a commitment believe these comments to be true. It's best not to go into something trying to change someone's mind about what he or she is looking for. It will save you from wasting your time if you only court people looking for the same level of commitment that you are.

What are your Courtship partner's views on gender roles?

Do they believe that all men are cheaters or that all women are gold diggers? Find out what they truly feel about the opposite sex. Do they believe a woman's place is in the home? Are you willing to take the role as homemaker if things get serious? Does your partner believe that the man should always pay for dates? Are you willing to pick up the tab every time? Does your partner view one gender as superior? What are their real views on chivalry? What about feminism? Make sure your partners personal views on gender are in line with your personal views.

What is your Courtship philosophy on life?
Does they see the glass half full or half empty? Does he believe it's him or her against the world? Does he or she believe the world revolves around their wants and needs? Is your partner committed to improving the lives of others? Do they want to live a life of material abundance or does he prefer a life of simplicity? You should know if you and your Courtship partner have similar values and world views before investing too much time in each other.

What is your Courtship partner's religious background and current belief system?
Was your partner raised with religion? If so, which religion and which denomination? What are their current religious beliefs? Does your Courtship partner believe there is one God, multiple gods or no God at all? Do they worship alone or with a congregation? How often do they worship? Does he or she prefer to be with someone with similar religious beliefs? If you and your significant other clash on religious and spiritual issues it can cause discord throughout the entire relationship. Figure these issues out early on.

What are your Courtship partner's political leanings?
It is not necessary to agree on every political issue in order to have a successful relationship but there are certain things you should agree on. What are your Courtship partner's views on abortion? Would it be a viable option if the two of you had an unwanted pregnancy? Do they approve of other forms of contraception, if so what kinds? What are their views on the right to bear arms? Does he or she own guns? How do you feel about that? You should explore your partner's views on any other political issue that is particularly important to you.

What are your Courtship partner's views on people with different lifestyles or ethnic backgrounds?

If you and your partner have wildly different opinions on race, class or sexuality it could cause conflict. Find out what is their general opinion of people who are of a different race? Is your partner tolerant of people with different religious beliefs? How do they feel about affirmative action? What about same sex marriage? Do they believe that the United States is superior to all other countries? Or does he or she have an allegiance to a different country? How do they feel about those who are less fortunate? Do they resent the top 1%? It is wise to find out about your partners prejudices early on so that you can make a well reasoned decision on it, if he or she is the right person for you.

On the first few courtship outings try to keep your nerves at bay by not worrying too much about trying to impress them but instead focus on getting to know the person you are with. Try not to be overly flattered by their compliments and don't become prematurely attached because the two of you love the same sports team. Get to know what kind of person your courtship partner is and if he or she is the kind of person you want to continue to invest time and energy in. While getting to know them remember to enjoy yourself and the person you are with even if you realize that it is not the perfect match. Each courtship is an opportunity to learn more about yourself and what you are looking for. Make the best of each interaction.

Is the person your best friend or at least becoming so?

It is easy to find a lover. It is easy to get excited about a new person. But if you cannot say that the person you are considering marrying has become or is becoming your best friend, you need to figure out why before you decide to marry. This is probably the single most overlooked question among couples, especially young ones.

And for good reason. Many people cannot not answer this in the affirmative. But you have to answer it. Over time, friendship is the greatest bond between a couple. If the person you marry does not become your best friend, you will either seek someone who will be or simply drift apart.

What is a best friend? Someone you can and do tell just about everything to. Someone you want to be with as much as possible. And someone you need. One of the most devastating ideas of the last generation was that needing or depending upon another person is a sign of weakness. The opposite is true. The inability to need is a sign of weakness -- you are afraid to relinquish power or afraid to be hurt.

Is there chemistry between the two of you?

As essential as being best friends and enjoying each other are, there should be a physical component to your relationship. Dating for marriage is not an interview for a platonic best friend. Nearly always, a woman who dates a man who meets the criteria listed here can grow to find him sexually attractive. If that were not the case, the majority of men would never attract a woman. There are very few men who turn heads. Most men become physically attractive to a woman thanks to other, masculine, qualities that they possess.

Does the person have a number of good friends and at least one very close friend of the same sex?

It is a bad sign if the person you are thinking of marrying does not have good friends (including of long duration) of the same sex.

Something is very wrong. This alone should rule out the person from consideration. A woman who cannot hold female friends and a man who cannot hold male friends have issues that will probably sink your marriage.

How does the person treat others?
It should go without saying that if the person is not kind to you, quit while you can. But it is far from sufficient that the person you are considering marrying treats you kindly. Watch how he or she treats waitresses, employees, family members and anyone else he/she comes into contact with. We promise you how the person treats others now is how this person will treat you later.

What problems do the two of you now have? And what inner voice of doubt, if any, are you suppressing?
Here is a rule that is rarely broken: Whatever problems you have before the wedding day, you will have during your marriage. Do not think that marrying will solve any problem you have with the person. You therefore have three choices: Make peace with the problem, see if it can be solved before deciding to marry, or don't marry the person. It is imperative that you be ruthlessly honest with yourself. And that is very hard. Nothing in life is easier than denying problems when you are in love. That is why it is important to pay attention to inner doubts.

How often do you fight?
It may be normal for couples to fight (though the ratio of loving moments to fights must be high to sustain a loving relationship). But it is usually a bad sign if you are doing so with any frequency while courting. Presumably that should be the easiest time to get along -- no children together, no joint financial problems, and the excitement of a new person.
If you do fight, do you quickly make up? Does he / she fight fairly and hear your side? Has either of you said "I'm sorry" after a fight?

And perhaps most important, do you fight over the same issue(s) with no resolution?

Do you share values?

Opposites attract in the very beginning. Likes stay together for the long term. The more you share, especially values, the better your chances of a good marriage. For example, if you think television watching is a form of self abuse and your prospective spouse loves watching for hours a day, you may have a big problem. Likewise if you have opposing political and social views to which you are passionately committed. Love conquers all pre-maritally. Not post.

Do you miss the person when you are not together?

This even holds true for men. Yes, men are better at being distracted by work, sports, computer games, the opposite sex, and God knows what else, but it is not a good sign if you rarely miss her when not together. As for women, if you don't miss him, it is probably a really bad sign.

Is the person unhappy?

Suffice it to say that the importance of marrying an essentially happy person cannot be exaggerated. If you are basically happy, do not think for a moment that you can make an unhappy person happy by marrying him or her. On the contrary, the ability of the unhappy to make the happy unhappy is far greater than the ability of the happy to make the unhappy happy.

What do people you respect think of the person you're considering marrying?

Young people are certain they know better than anyone else in the world what is good for them. So a lack of enthusiasm for the person you are considering for marriage on the part of family or friends may mean little or nothing. And sometimes family objections should mean little or nothing. But if objections come, let us say, from a parent you respect for reasons that are not easily dismissed, and if others you respect are unenthusiastic as well, you should take the objections seriously. You would do so regarding the purchase of a car, wouldn't you? Yet no car will affect your life nearly as much as your spouse.

Will honest answers help you marry well or avoid a marriage that can make your life miserable? There is an easy way to find out. Ask any married or divorced person who will open up to you whether these questions need to be answered. They are the experts. Not the never-married, like you, who usually know nothing about marriage.

You'll never know everything about the person you've chosen to marry. But the more information you have before entering into this commitment, the less chance you will be confronted with unfulfillable expectations.

Do Your Emotional Work

It is good to do as much of your emotional work now before you marry rather than dumping a lot of unvoiced expectations upon your partner after the marriage. You don't want to set your marriage up for future problems and maybe even possible failure because expectations were never given a voice.

As couples, we enter into marriage from two different vantage points. We come from two different background experiences, which contribute to differing expectations. That in itself, can lend itself to future clashes. It's good to try to learn what you can (without living together first) so you can work through many of your differences before you marry. (There will be many, many more that you won't be able to work through beforehand. So eliminate what you can while you're preparing for marriage.)

Keep in Mind:

It's better to find out your differences now before you marry. That way you can decide if it truly is best for you to marry. It would be better to part ways now than it would be to have a failed marriage —especially with children involved. Asking each other the right questions and then working through the truthful answers, could help you to better know your compatibility.

Now is also a good time to learn the skill of building communication bridges together in mature ways. You will be thankful you did. As you go through the questions, work through any disagreements in ways that help your relationship grow stronger. This will take effort and intentionality to do this.

For some reason your first marriage didn't work out. Before you consider a second or third time around at **"happily ever after,"** here are some things to consider before you walk down the aisle again:

You're Still You. You are the common denominator in all of your relationships. You can pick a new partner, but whatever issues you had that played a part in the downfall of your first marriage are likely to be a problem in your second (or third) marriage, too -- unless you resolve them. Make sure you really uncover why you made the choices you made in your first marriage, and be fearless in taking responsibility for the things you might have done differently. The good news is that by gently holding yourself accountable for your mistakes, you'll find you get access to the power to change.

Think Practice, Not Perfect. The good news about second and third marriages is that you actually do have the opportunity to get it right -- or at least 'righter' -- this time. You've learned a lot in your first marriage about your strengths, your weaknesses, and what does -- or does not -- work for you. Second (and third) marriages allow you to take everything you learned, and use it to choose a partner who is a better match. But no marriage -- and no person -- is going to be perfect. So look at marriage as a practice -- think of love as something you do, not something you feel. And your relationship is the gym where you get to go every day to "work out". Yes, we know it can be painful and sometimes even boring -- but you can only get out of something what you put into it. So why not do the work?

Children are a Very Big Deal. Nothing torpedoes a second or third marriage like conflicts over the children. His, hers, and yours together. Be realistic! Don't expect everyone to get along all the time, or even much of the time. Understand that your new spouse's children most likely prefer their old family system to this new one -- after all, they didn't just fall in love with someone new! -- and that's not a reflection on you. Even if they think it is! So don't take it personally. (Easier said than done, I know.) You can also take a spiritual approach by helping children understand that nothing in life is ever permanent -- that's a lesson we all learn sooner or later. Let them know you understand that divorce meant learning that difficult lesson earlier in life than they wanted to. Be compassionate with their struggle and things will go as smoothly as they can -- even if they're not all that smooth!

Remember, a Second Marriage Is a Merger. If first marriages are like starting a business from scratch -- second marriages are like merging two companies that already have assets, liabilities, and human resource policies. You can't expect your prospective spouse -- and his or her children, if there are any -- to just seamlessly adopt your way of doing things. For this reason, a second or third marriage is far more challenging! No one -- and by no one, I mean you -- is going to be getting their way all, or even most, of the time. You have to think of marriage as a sort of service project -- where if everyone gives 100%, there will be more than enough to go around. And if you are marrying someone who doesn't view a relationship this way, think loooong and hard before marrying them.

Take Your Time. Obviously, the best way to prevent a divorce is by not getting into a weak marriage in the first place. This is so obvious no one does it! Slow down. We know from experience that wanting to hurry down the aisle is sometimes the best predictor of a relationship that is in trouble. In fact, if something seems urgent, we say don't do it. No one should ever get married under pressure, or because time is running out. A great relationship will be great whether the two people involved get married, or not. So take your time to talk over all the details. Really dive into the areas where conflict is likely to occur: like sex, money, the children. Try to prevent problems before they start, or deal with them before they get too big. Because there's no problem so big that it can't get worse after you're married!

It's crucial to learn what you did or didn't do in your last marriage that might have been part of the reason for it ending. Consider things like, how did I communicate? What could I have done differently in my last marriage? How much energy did I put into nurturing our love? Was I more of a giver or taker? What makes me happy in a relationship? These internal questions will begin to help you identify what YOU can do to insure that the next marriage works.

Discuss the tough questions: Chances are there are children in the mix as well as exes and ex in-laws! Often, couples avoid talking about how they will create a wonderful marriage amidst the challenges of instant families and exes. Ask each other questions like, "Will we or how will we discipline each other's children? What will be the rules for both of our children in our new home? What kind of relationship will each of us have with our exes? Is your spouse going to be spending time alone with his/her ex to discuss the children and how do you feel about that?

What has my potential spouse learned from his/her previous marriage? Hopefully, you've done the work of learning how to create a better relationship than your last one. Has the person you want to marry done the same? What does he/she say is the reason for the divorce and does he/she take any responsibility for it? What does your potential spouse wish to change this time around?

Call upon your parents: It really makes sense that our parents modeled marriage for us and if it wasn't a great model, you will be especially challenged at creating a great marriage. Yes, you say you want to have a great marriage but we don't always do what we say even when we know its good for us (have you been eating healthy every day of your life? We didn't think so). If your parents' marriage wasn't a good example for you, know that you need to pay special attention to learn how good marriages work. Read books, visit the web, get therapy, or do all of these to learn more about how you will get it right this time around.

Create a relationship where both of you have TIME for each other: Successful marriages have one simple secret, they are actively being in love. They don't assume love will sustain itself just because they fell in love. They prioritize their marriage on a daily basis. My research showed that happy couples reported spending a daily average of 30 minutes of uninterrupted time talking with their spouse as compared to unhappy couples who spent much less. Discuss with your potential mate before marriage how you will prioritize your love and make sure it's already happening at the stage before you decide to make a lifelong commitment Just like everything else in life that you want to have success in (parenting, career), marriage takes focus and energy to create the special bond you deserve. The second marriage starts off with so many people and things pulling at it. You need a plan to secure alone time for the two of you. The good news is that your next marriage gives you the opportunity to get it right and have what you've wanted in a loving relationship. But like anything else that is wonderful in your life, it doesn't just happen. You make it happen. All of the questions above don't have a right or wrong answer. Rather, it's the process of discussing them and finding resolution that will avoid great conflict and make your marriage work. When you're in love, your energy affect each other constantly. Learn what puts a smile on your lover's face and remember to do that. Love builds on itself when you are focused and nurturing.

How to Talk to Someone You Are Interested in:

Be More Memorable: How to Better Answer the 3 Questions You Always Get Asked When Meeting Someone New

Almost every time you meet someone new, there are three questions you will probably have to answer during your conversation:

What's your name?
What do you do?
Where are you from?

These three questions are so common, and you answer them so frequently, that it is very easy to get in the habit of answering them the same way, again and again, without thinking. You probably get bored with your own answers, so you don't put energy and effort into offering them in an interesting way. "Hi, I'm Joe. I work in public relations for an energy company downtown, and I'm from the Midwest but moved here a couple years ago." Zzzzz...
You might even feel like Bill Murray's character in Groundhog Day – going through the exact same routine time in and time out. It may even contribute to why so many of us dread meeting new people. Yet it's worth upping your game in this area; how you respond to these three common introductory questions can greatly impact your first impression, how memorable you are to a new acquaintance, and whether your relationship ever gets past first base, so to speak.
We will outline 6 specific strategies for answering these almost inescapable questions in ways that are distinct and memorable. I will also share advice from experts in communications, linguistics, and networking about how you can stand out from the pack. Additionally, we will give specific examples of how you can use these tips in practice. First, let's take a look at what those strategies are:
6 Ways to Make Your Answers More Memorable

Here's a quick snapshot of the ways you can make your answers to these three common questions more memorable:

Repeat Your Answer. Science and common experience tell us that repeating a thing makes it more memorable. So find subtle ways to repeat your answers, without making it obvious what you are doing.

Ask a Question. People are more likely to absorb and retain new information if their brain is engaged, which is what happens when you ask a person you've just met a question.

Tell a Story. We're all drawn to a good story. Use relevant, brief anecdotes or quick stories to stand out. Just don't be that guy or gal who launches into their entire life story within the first two minutes of an introduction.

Be Clear and Avoid Trying to Be Overly Clever. Always choose clarity. When you are meeting someone for the first time, you should be cautious about trying to be overly clever in your answers to these questions.

Create a Personal Association. A great way to be memorable is to create an association between your answers to the three questions and something that is more memorable to the person you are talking to. To use a quick example: a person you just met is more likely to remember your name if you share a name with someone in their family. Find ways to leverage these connections.

Find Your Inner Black Sheep. Look for ways to describe yourself that highlights your uniqueness. Be different if you want to be remembered. Vanilla is boring and forgettable; Cherry Garcia, with cherries and chocolate chunks, is memorable. Mmmmm...Cherry Garcia. Where were we?

Now, let's see how these strategies apply to each of the three common questions:

How to Answer **"What's Your Name?"** in a Memorable Way
Repeat Your Name – Without Being Obvious About It
When telling someone your name for the first time, one of the best ways to help them remember it is by repeating your name in a subtle way. One of the reasons people often have trouble remembering names is because saying it just once makes it unlikely the name will move from that person's short-term memory, or their "working memory," to their long-term memory.

If you want to make your name memorable by repeating it, but you don't want to be obvious about it, then try these approaches:

Use your name in dialogue. You might say, **"So my friend says to me, 'John, you put the paper on backwards again...'"**

Address yourself by name. Try this in conversation: "I was really frustrated, but I said to myself, John, you're going to **learn how to speak Jive** if it kills you."

Explain the origin of your name, especially if it is unusual. If you have an unusual or hard to pronounce name, you might try explaining briefly the history or origin of your name so you can repeat it. For example, I might say, "Corcoran comes from the Latin, Corcorinitus, which means, **'tries too hard to be funny.'"**

Tell a Story
Another way to make your name memorable is to tell a story, such as how you got your name.

For example, my first name is John, which isn't very memorable. However, I was named after my grandfather, a B-17 pilot during WWII. If I meet you and I explain this background and tell a quick story about my grandfather, you are more likely to remember my name.

The author's grandfather, John H. Corcoran Sr., a B-17 pilot during WWII.

Or, let's say your name is Steve, and it turns out your parents named you after Steve McQueen, the actor. Because they had a sense of humor.

You might tell a short story about it: **"My dad was a huge fan of Steve McQueen's movies back when I was born. My mom was dead set against it, but they made a deal where he got to name me Steve, and she got to name my sister Anne, after the character in her favorite book, Anne of Green Gables."**

Create a Personal Association

Another way to make your name memorable is to create an association between your name and something that is more memorable to the person you are talking to.

For example, if you say your name is "Mitch" and the person you are talking to says, **"I have an uncle named Mitch,"** you could ask a number of questions about Uncle Mitch so that the person you have just met makes a firm connection between you and their uncle.

You can also connect your name with something the person you have just met already knows. Here are a few examples:

I have an unusual last name, which most people have trouble spelling. When I lived in Washington D.C., I would say I was **"John Corcoran, spelled like the Corcoran Gallery,"** an art museum near the White House. I think some people may have wondered whether I was heir to some Corcoran Gallery fortune, which probably made me even more memorable. (I also think that's what got me a first date with my wife.) By creating an association between my last name and the Corcoran Gallery – a name which most people in Washington D.C. already know – I increased the chances my unusual last name would be memorable.

Amanda Marko, a strategic communications expert, tells a story about this approach. **"So, my husband's name is Nick Marko, and people say to him all the time, 'I bet you got teased about Marco Polo a lot as a kid.'** And he always says, **'Yeah, I did...until the kids got a little older and realized what Nick rhymes with.'"**

How to Answer "What Do You Do?" in a Memorable Way
Ask a Question

If you want someone you just met to remember what you do, a great approach is to ask a question that forces them to think. Art of Manliness style expert Antonio Centeno uses this approach to explain what he does for a living, which has evolved from custom clothier to creating online courses and videos which help men to dress better.

"When people ask what I do, I usually flip the question and say, 'You know how most guys don't dress very well?'" says Centeno. This usually gets the person he is talking to nodding along. **"Then I talk about how I solve that problem. I might mention that I have a 9-year-old, and let's say I go to take him to the doctor. Now imagine a guy comes in who is wearing a Grateful Dead t-shirt, shorts and flip-flops. Am I going to give my kid to this person? Probably not. Now imagine a guy wearing a white lab coat walks in. Everyone can relate to how clothing can make a huge difference."**

When you force the person you are talking with to think by asking a question, and to relate what you do to their own life, they are far more likely to remember you.

Be Clear and Avoid Trying to Be Overly Clever

Derek Coburn wears multiple hats. He's a financial advisor for high net-worth individuals, he's an entrepreneur, and he's an author of the great book **Networking Is Not Working**.

Explaining all of these roles can be confusing. **"Often times we get caught up in trying to be clever and it ends up not communicating what we do,"** says Coburn. Instead, Coburn recommends keeping things simple and relevant to the person you are talking to by starting with questions. **"By learning more about the person I am talking to first and what they do, I'm in a better spot to lead with what's more relevant to the conversation."**

Naveen Dittakavi made the same mistake of trying to be too creative in describing what he does when he founded his own **software consulting firm**. **"When I first started consulting, I** didn't know where I fit in the mix – I arbitrarily took a title for myself of 'software architect.' But no one knew what that meant."

Worse yet, Dittakavi found many people thought he was an employee rather than a business owner. Eventually, Dittakavi settled on a way of describing what he does. He started saying, **"I'm Naveen and I run a web development company,"** and he found that people he met were far more likely to understand him – and to remember him as well.

How to Answer **"Where Are You From?"** in a Memorable Way

When answering where you are from, your answer will always be relative. If you're standing in Miami, it is memorable to say you're from New York City. If you're in Manhattan, you need to be more specific.

But the best approach is to find a way of explaining where you are from that is distinct. In other words, to describe where you live that makes you seem like a black sheep in a sea of white sheep.

Antonio Centeno does this beautifully. On the surface, Centeno appears pretty clean cut. He's a former Marine with short-cropped hair and no unusual facial hair or visible tattoos. You might even say he could blend into a crowd.

But it's all in how you spin it.

Antonio is actually a heterosexual male style expert who runs his fashion empire out of his hometown, in tiny Wittenberg, Wisconsin. Population? 1,113 people. Now that is a little more memorable.

When Antonio tells people where he's from, he makes a point of mentioning his hometown's population because *"my town is incredibly small for most people. I'm an oddity because people think with a fashion company, I would live in New York or Los Angeles or Chicago."*

He could say he's from Wisconsin and leave it at that. But highlighting how small his hometown is makes him far more memorable.

Antonio finds his uniqueness means people are more likely to remember him, and they're more likely to later tell their brother or husband or father to check out his website, Real Men Real Style. *"Many times I'll get an email from someone a few weeks after we've met saying you were brought up in a conversation,"* says Centeno.

Go Out and Be Memorable

Hopefully these strategies gave you some ideas for making yourself more memorable the next time you meet someone new and need to answer the world's most common introductory questions.
And remember: if you try these strategies and people still can't remember you, you can always move to a small town in rural Wisconsin, because that is really memorable. I'm sure Antonio would enjoy the company.
How do you describe yourself in a memorable way when you meet someone new?

The Questions you should ask, or be aware of, before you say, "I do"

You're thinking about spending the rest of your life with that special person. But do you really know them as well as you think? Are there areas you need to know about (or they need to know about you) that you haven't discussed? The best time to get down to the nitty-gritty with each other is before you say, "I do." You need to know what to expect after the wedding day, and to decide if you really want to spend the rest of your life with this person the way they are now. Chances are they (and you) won't change that much, so if you really want to know who you are agreeing to love, work through these questions together. There's no hurry — take all the time you need. But there's one rule. You must be completely, gut-wrenchingly honest! If you misrepresent yourself, they will remember.

Past
The best part about my childhood was?
The worst part about my childhood was?
The scariest thing that ever happened to me was?
Something I'm afraid to tell anyone about my past is?
A past situation that could affect my future is?
I've had [ ] sexual partners before this relationship.
The way I feel about my past relationship history is?

Who I Am
My biggest needs in life are?
My most frequent mood is?
The thing I hate most is?
The thing I worry about most is?
Three things I want to change about myself are?
Three things I really like about myself are?
My most common daydream is?
I get angry when?
My favorite kind of house pet is?

My overall opinion about myself is?

I think my greatest personality asset is?

My greatest personality weakness is?

I find the greatest enjoyment in?

The sin I struggle most with is?

I'm most ashamed about?

Someone I greatly admire is?

The way I feel about death is?

I think war is?

I feel happy when?

I have no use for people who?

When someone acts rude to me, I?

When someone is unfair, I?

I feel jealous of?

My dream vacation would include?

The things I find the most fun are?

My favorite sport(s) is?

Playing sports in my future is a [ ] on a scale from one to ten.

Watching sports on T.V. is a [ ] for me on a scale from one to ten.

I am disgusted by?

When I am afraid (substitute sad, angry, happy, lonely, tired), I?

My hobbies include?

I spend [ ] hours a week at my hobbies.

What I really want when I am sick is?

The part of my body I am most bothered by is?

The part of my body I am most happy with is?

What hurts me most is?

The best (and worst) thing about life is?

The first thing I notice about someone is?

When someone is angry with me, I?

When someone is disappointed in me, I?

The worst (and best) thing about the opposite sex is

Being teachable means?

People (including me) should say they're sorry when?

Marriage My reasons for wanting to get married are?

I think the keys to a good marriage are?

The biggest mistakes I made in past relationships are?
The area I've grown the most in relationships is?
Relationships in the past have taught me?
I've always viewed marriage as?
My parents had a [ ] marriage.
I learned [ ] about marriage from my parents.
I think the things in marriage you should be honest about are?
The areas I'm concerned about being married are?
The areas I'm excited about being married are?
Marriage for me will be giving up?
Marriage for me will be gaining?
I think separate vacations are?
Traveling together is?
When having conflict, I like to: cool off by myself before discussing the problem; discuss and work the problem out right away; pretend there is no problem and just move on; analyze the problem as to what it is, why it happened, how to avoid it in the future, etc?
Arguing and or fighting is?
The best way to handle disagreements is to?
What I fear most about marriage is?
What I anticipate most about marriage is?
The role of in-laws in marriage is?
The thing that will make me most secure (and insecure) in marriage is?
Dating (each other) after you are married is?
Love is?
"Till death do us part" means?
I think people should be allowed to divorce when?
For me, divorce is?

Money Finances
I think money is?
Spending money is hard/easy for me because?
The biggest waste of money is?
The best investment of money is?
I have [ ] in personal debt.

I use credit cards for?
I think car loans are?
Saving up to buy big ticket items is?
My savings plan is?
My retirement plan is?
The way I feel about tithing is?
I hope my spouse is a: saver, spender, somewhere in between.
On a scale from one to ten, financial security is [ ] in importance to me.
I want to save up to buy a?
The kind of house I want to own someday is?
Other items I hope to own are?
Charities I want to contribute to are?

Physical Appearance

Is my own appearance important to me?
Is it important that my spouse maintains his/her current physical appearance/weight throughout our marriage?
How important is hygiene to me, i.e. brushing teeth, taking showers, deodorant, etc.?
How do I like to dress for special occasions? For church? For dates? For work?
Do I want to be able to have a say in my spouse's choice of clothing, hairstyle, or general appearance?
Do I care if they have a say in mine?
Is cologne/perfume important to me?
What physical features are attractive to me?

Household

How clean is a home that is comfortable for me?
What is my favorite thing about home?
What can I not tolerate in my home (noise, clutter, dirt, pets, unmade beds, etc.)?
How many/which jobs do I think I should do to keep my house maintained?

How many/which jobs do I think my spouse should do around the house?
Who should keep the yard maintained (spouse, both, or hired out)?
Who will maintain the cars (spouse, both, or hired out)?
Who will make decisions for and carry out decorating the home (spouse, both, hired out)?
Who will cook family meals?
How many meals do I expect to cook or for my spouse to cook daily?
Who will do the shopping?
Who will do laundry?
Who will do the dishes?
Who will pay bills?

Recreation
My idea of recreation is?
To me, camping means?
My favorite sports are?
The way I relax on the weekends is by?
What areas of recreation do I want my spouse to accompany me on?
What areas of recreation do I want to do with my friends or alone?
How often will I want to spend time away from the family in my own recreation?

Children
I think children are?
Children get on my nerves when they?
I love it when children?
The way I feel about other people's children is?
The way children usually feel about me is?
Children should be disciplined when?
The way I want to discipline my children is?
The role of a parent is?
I want [ ] children someday.
How important is showing physical affection to my children?

Is telling my children I love them important?
How much time do I think I should spend with my children daily?
How important is two-parent interaction and discipline?
I think the bottom line for discipline should be with the (mom or dad)?
How important is it for children to respect their parents in my home?
When it comes to discipline, I think I will be: lenient, strict, or somewhere in-between?
Where do I want my children educated (private school, Christian school, home school, etc.)?

Health & History
Taking care of myself and my health is [ ] important to me.
I think a healthy lifestyle includes?
Physical exercise is?
To me, eating right means?
My idea of a good work out is?
My life fitness plan is to?
My health problems (present or past) are?
I take medication for?
I think life long-term supports are?
People in my family have a history of the following health problems?
People in my family have died at the ages of?

Work
My idea of a dream job is?
I think the average number of hours a person can regularly work a week and maintain family commitment is?
Providing for the family is whose responsibility?
My career plans are?
How important is a steady job to me?
What kind of work ethic do I want in my mate?
Where do I draw the line with a job that demands too much time?
My plans for retirement are?

Determining A Person's Spiritual Life:

What do you understand to be God's purposes/priorities for the Church / Mosque?

What do you see as the man's role in the local Church Mosque? Your own role?

What do you see as your wife's role in local Church / Mosque Ministry?

How would those who know you well describe your personal character?

Are you faithful in Church / Mosque attendance/participation? How long have you been a member of your current fellowship?

Does one of us have an individual spiritual practice? Is the practice and the time devoted to it acceptable to the other? Does each partner understand and respect the other's choices?

What are your habits with regard to prayer?

What are your habits with regard to study of the Bible and Holy Qur'an?

What would you say is your spiritual gift(s)?

What are your spiritual strengths?

What is your father's understanding of Christianity / Islam? How would you describe your father's personal character?

What is your mother's understanding of Christianity / Islam? How would you describe your mother's personal character?

Recognizing we are all imperfect, in what one or two areas do you think God wants you to improve most?

Do you have a teachable spirit? Can you cite any examples?

How important is it to be part of a small accountability/support group?

What is the importance of music in life and worship?

What are your daily personal devotional practices? (Prayer, reading, meditation, memorization)

What would our family devotions look like? Who leads out in this?

The way I feel about God is?

I think the way God feels about me is?

On a scale of one to ten, going to Church or Mosque is [ ] in importance for my life and future.

I want to raise my kids in the [ ] faith.

Will God be the center of my home? Why or why not?
If yes, how will I make Him the center?

Prayer is something I do when?

To me, the Bible is?

Select and discuss the following.
To me, God is: personal, real, distant, vague, angry, happy, loving, harsh, demanding, gentle, kind, good, make-believe, living, powerful, weak, or other.

The way to have a relationship with God is?

For me, including God in my daily life is?

On a scale from one to ten, obeying God and His word is a [ ] to me.

When I die, I?

Determining How I will Be Treated in this Relationship:

How do you define forever, forgiveness and fidelity? Very important question, maybe the most important. You want to know if your partner is planning on being with you (and only you) forever. You also want to know if they will be quick to forgive when you have disagreements, the operative word being quick.

What will you look like in 20 years? Another great question, you don't want to wait until your partner has put on an additional 100 pounds to discuss your personal preferences. Prior to getting married, discuss your preferences with your spouse. You also want to discuss how you will both achieve, and or maintain the results that you're looking for.

Determining A Person's Financial Life: (Very serious, Money Questions)

What are your financial goals, aspirations, expectations and how will you achieve them? A majority of divorces occur due to stress on the relationship related to finances. Having financial goals are beneficial to the success of a marriage relationship, so be sure to ask this question. You don't want wait until you've been married for five years to discover that your partner has no financial goals or aspirations.

What percentage of our income are we prepared to spend to purchase and maintain our home on a monthly or annual basis?

Not that you can perfectly predict the future, but what working hours are you comfortable with? Also, when are we planning to retire? You want to know if your spouse will be working all the time, so that you all can plan accordingly. Also, don't forget to discuss your retirement plans; you will appreciate these questions as you get older.

What is our ultimate financial goal regarding annual income, and when do we anticipate achieving it? By what means and through what efforts?

Who is responsible for keeping our house and yard cared for and organized? Are we different in our needs for cleanliness and organization?

How much money do we earn together? Now? In one year? In five years? Ten? Who is responsible for which portion? Now? In one year? Five? Ten?

What are our categories of expense (rent, clothing, insurance, travel)? How much do we spend monthly, annually, in each category? How much do we *want* to be able to spend?

How much time will each of us spend at work, and during what hours? Do we begin work early? Will we prefer to work into the evening?

If one of us doesn't want to work, under what circumstances, if any, would that be okay?

What justifies going into debt?

Do you feel stress when facing financial problems? How do you deal with that stress?

How often do you use credit cards, and what do you buy with them?

How should we prepare for a financial emergency?

Do you feel that lack of money is a good reason not to have children?

Will we have a budget?

How do you feel about helping me pay my debts?

What are your feelings about saving money?

Do you prefer separate bank accounts or assets in different names? Why?

How ambitious are you? Are we comfortable with the other's level of ambition?

Who will handle the money?

How many credit cards will we have?

How much money will we save from each paycheck?

Do you believe that our parents should know our financial condition, whether good or bad, just because they want to? How far should this go?

Determining A Person's Family Life Aptitude

What place does the other's family play in *our* family life? How often do we visit or socialize together? If we have out-of-town relatives, will we ask them to visit us for extended periods? How often?

If we have children, what kind of relationship do we hope our parents will have with their grandchildren? How much time will they spend together?

Will we have children? If so, when? How many? How important is having children to each of us?

How will having a child change the way we live now? Will we want to take time off from work, or work a reduced schedule? For how long? Will we need to rethink who is responsible for housekeeping?

Are we satisfied with the quality and quantity of friends we currently have? Would we like to be more involved socially? Are we overwhelmed socially and need to cut back on such commitments?

Do we eat meals together? Which ones? Who is responsible for the food shopping? Who prepares the meals? Who cleans up afterward?

Is each of us happy with the other's approach to health? Does one have habits or tendencies that concern the other (e.g., smoking, excessive dieting, poor diet)?

If "your"daughter were marrying "you," what cautions would you have?

If "your" son were marrying "you," what cautions would you have?

Determining A Person's Other Relationships

What influence, if any, will your family have on our marriage? It's probably a good idea to find out if you're mother-in-law is going to be making all of the important decisions in your marriage, or if her opinion will strongly influence your life.

Describe your relationship with your father? Was (is) it honoring? Was (is) it obedient?

Do any mental or emotional illnesses that could affect your children run in your family?

Describe your relationship with your mother? Was (is) it honoring? Was (is) it obedient?

How many siblings do you have? What are their names, ages, cities of residence? Can you describe your relationship with each of your siblings?

Can you describe your relationship with your grandparents?

Can you describe your relationship with your friends?

What are my partner's needs for cultivating or maintaining friendships outside our relationship? Is it easy for me to support those needs, or do they bother me in any way?

Have you ever been peer-dependent? How did you resist this?

Are you consistently faithful in fulfilling your commitments? Give examples.

Do you show a regular willingness to serve others? In what ways?

In what ways is self-centeredness expressed in your life?

How do you relate to authority in your life? If so, what adjectives would your employers use to describe you?

Have you ever been a supervisor? If so, what adjectives would your employees use to describe you?

Are you ever manipulative of others?

What kinds of situations cause you frustration? How do you respond?

What circumstances might make you impatient or angry? How do you handle anger? Have you ever been violent? Do you raise your voice when angry?

Have you ever had to deal with a broken relationship? If so, please provide the details of that relationship, how long ago, the situation, and how did you handle it?

How much time do you plan spending with your friends after we get married; what is your relationship with friends of the opposite sex? These are good questions, the best answer maybe found by looking to see what your partner is currently doing. When you get married they won't be a brand new person, you will both be the exact same people, with the exact same relationships and thoughts. Be sure to openly discuss the time you will spending with both your male and female friends, and the importance or relative unimportance of those relationships.

Determining A Person's Personal Habits Affecting Marriage

What are your beliefs regarding diet and How to Eat to Live Books 1 and 2?

Are your eating habits disciplined? Do you have any food dislikes?

Are you a vegetarian?

Do you have a weight problem?

Do you have any physical or mental disabilities or diseases? Any allergies? Prior or current health problems?

Do you drink alcohol? If so, what and how often? What are your views on alcohol?

Do you smoke? What are your views on smoking?

Are your spending habits disciplined? Do you tithe? What is your view of debt?

How would you describe your work ethic? Do you have a high standard of excellence? Do you tend to be either slothful or a workaholic? How many hours per week do you work?

Do you travel with your job? If so, how often? Do you see this changing in your future?

If a relocation were offered to you by an employer, would you consider it? What would you weigh when considering such a move?

What is your discipline in studying?

Do you read regularly, and if so, what? Who is your favorite author? Outside the Bible, what would be your five favorite non-fiction books? Five favorite fiction books?

What are your habits regarding sleeping? Are you lethargic? Are your sleep habits irregular?

Do you follow a regular schedule? Are you organized?

Would you consider yourself neat or messy?

What is your practice regarding personal prayer?

What is your level of personal cleanliness and hygiene?

Do you have any personal habits that might annoy others?

Determining A Person's Understanding of Marital Roles

If you already subscribe to the concept of courtship, give me your definition of it.

Do you tend to be more of a leader or follower in life? Can you cite any examples?

In making decisions, what role does God's Word play?

What is your attitude toward women? What is their purpose?

What is your view on the role of a wife?

What are your views on women working outside the home?

What are your views concerning divorce and remarriage?

Can you tell me your thoughts on how a man should provide for a wife and family?

Can you tell me your thoughts on how a man should protect a wife and children?

How do you see your future relationship with your in-laws working out?
What has been your prior experience with dating and romance?

Have you ever kissed or been physically intimate in any way with a Girl / Woman?
If so, explain the circumstances.

Have you ever kissed or been physically intimate in any way with a Boy / Man?
If so, explain the circumstances.

What is your stand on abortion? What about in the case of rape?

How do you relate to children? How often are you around children?

What are your thoughts regarding birth control and family planning?

How many children do you hope to have?

What is your attitude toward adopting children?

What are your views on child training, including corporal punishment?

What are your views on homeschooling?

What are your thoughts on family worship? What would be the key attributes of such a practice in your home?

When you fail someone, what actions do you take to rectify the situation?

Are you honest? Do you ever slant the truth for your own benefit? How have you prepared yourself for marriage?

In what ways do you think you may need to grow before marriage? What does "leave and cleave" mean to you? Are you prepared to put your wife first, before all others, including your parents? Give me an example of what this may look like to you.

Determining A Person's Moral Standards

What are your standards of propriety in dress? How do you dress?

Describe your standards of dress for women?

What are your views on head coverings for women?

What are your views on public swimming?

Do you use offensive language?

Do you watch television, R-rated movies? PG-rated movies? What were the last five movies you watched?

What kind of music do you prefer? What kind of music would you find offensive?

Have you ever been exposed to pornography? If so, explain the extent and the circumstances.

Have you ever been exposed to homosexuality? If so, explain the extent and the circumstances.

Do you currently use any type of drugs? Have you in your past? If so, explain the extent and the circumstances.

Do you have any financial debt? If so, explain the extent and the circumstances.

Have you ever been in trouble with the law? If so, explain the extent and the circumstances.

What tendencies do you have toward prejudice or racism?

Have you ever had periods of rebellion? If so, explain the extent and the circumstances. Are there any unsettled issues with your parents?

If I had bad breath or body odor or wear dirty clothes, will you tell me? Should I tell you? Why or why not? How should we do it?

What is nagging? Do I nag? How does it make you feel?

DO you approve without reservation of the way I dress?

What does my family do that annoys you?

Would it bother you if I made body noises all the time, like passing gas or burping?

Is there anything you do in your line of work that I would disapprove of or that would hurt me?

Do you believe that you should stick with a marriage if you are unhappy all the time?

When do you need space away from me?

Determining A Person's Future

Can you describe your life purpose, i.e., how you intend to use your interests, experiences, skills, and talents to serve and glorify God?

What role would your husband, wife and children play in your life purpose?

What role would your job/career play in your life purpose?

Where do you see yourself in 10 years? In 20 years?

Where do you see yourself spiritually in 10 years? In 20 years?

When God calls you to return to him, how would you like people to remember you?

Determining A Person's Expectations

It is not the all important questions such as do you see life as a glass half full, half empty, or do you ask if life has given you twice as much glass as you need? The question is **"what are the expectations?"**, do you fill the gas tank when it is half full, 3/4 down or wait until it is almost running on fumes? What will that mean next day when the other person is running late and finds a gas tank that they filled yesterday is now empty?

Do you have a personal timetable for marriage? If so, what is it?

What type of education are you hoping that your future wife will have? That your future husband will have?

Have we discussed our expectations for how the household will be maintained, and are we in agreement on who will manage the chores? Do you have the same expectations and standards?

What is the meaning of headship and submission in the Bible and Holy Qur'an and in our marriage?

What are expectations about situations where one of us might be alone with someone of the opposite sex?

How are tasks shared in the home: cleaning, cooking, washing dishes, yard work, car upkeep, repairs, shopping for food, and household stuff?

What are the expectations for togetherness?

What is an ideal non-special evening?

How do you understand who initiates sex and how often?

Who does the checkbook — or are there two?

Would you like the bed made... every day?

Wash clothes once a week or just when you run out of clean ones?

Balance the bank statement every month or only after you are notified your checks are bouncing?

List the five most important characteristics of a wife (for you personally).

List the five most important characteristics of a husband (for you personally).

List any characteristics or personality traits that would bother or irritate you in a wife.

Whenever we have difficult feelings about each other, should we
(1) remain silent,
(2) say something as soon as the difficult feelings arise,
(3) wait a certain amount of time before raising the issue, or
(4) do something else? If so, what?

If you always say you are going to do something but never do it, what is the most effective way to bring this problem to your attention?

What did you admire about the way your mother and father treated each other?

What is the best way for me to communicate difficult feelings about you so that you are not offended?

Who should know about the arguments we have?

What makes you not want to talk to me?

Do you feel you could communicate with me under any circumstance and about any subject?

Own a home or not? Why?

What kind of neighborhood? Why?

How many cars? New? Used?

View of money in general. How much to the Church? Mosque?

How do you make money decisions?

Where will you buy clothes: Department store? Thrift store? In between? Why?

How much money should we spend on entertainment?

How often should we eat out? Where?

What kind of vacations are appropriate and helpful for us?

How many toys? Snowmobile, boat, cabin?

Should we have a television? Where? What is fitting to watch? How much?

What are the criteria for movies and theater?

What will our guidelines be for the children?

Who is the main breadwinner?

Should the wife work outside the home? Before kids? With kids at home? After kids?

What are your views of daycare for children?

What determines where we will locate? Job? Whose job? Church? Family?

Determining A Person's Ability to Cope with Conflict

Of course you're in love. You know you're ready to vow "through sickness and health … until death do us part" – however, take a deep breath and consider these questions. How do I handle conflict? Am I willing to face the situation and discuss options, or do I ignore the facts and hope they will go away?

Some couples pleasantly coast through courting, get married, and then receive a shock when their first round of conflict hits. They are unaware that two imperfect people experience friction no matter how much they love each other. Conflict is an unavoidable part of life, and it can destroy a couple who hasn't learned how to properly resolve it.

It is important that you deal with conflict several times before considering engagement. Determine whether both of you have shown a desire to compromise in past arguments. If not, does one of you try to bully the other with angry outbursts? If you've had trouble handling disagreements, consider dating longer to learn how to disagree cooperatively. If nothing improves, you may need to end your relationship.

Civilized arguments can benefit a relationship by exposing neglect, unrealistic expectations, or different points of view. Sometimes, neither person is wrong. Each one is simply approaching the same topic from unique perspectives. Therefore, do not try to avoid conflict but seek to resolve it in a loving, mature manner. If you cannot freely voice your opinions, you will live in miserable bondage to another person. Both parties should have the freedom to express their ideas and desires.

A relationship devoid of conflict may signal that one of you is either too passive or too afraid to be genuine. These attitudes are not conducive to an intimate marriage, and you should not continue dating if you cannot be authentic with each other. Healthy relationships foster an environment in which you have the freedom to disagree. Thus, before you get engaged, make sure you both feel free to be yourselves and know how to lovingly resolve conflict.

Ask yourself honestly, can I talk about my **anger** or disappointment with my partner and can we reach a compromise? Can we come to an agreement about how to deal with our problems—a way to communicate that does not include violence, put-downs or walking away without resolving the issues?

Can they handle conflict?
Conflict is certain in marriage, but that's not all negative. Learning to resolve conflict can have many positive benefits, provided you learn how to handle conflict in a healthy way. Healthy conflict gives birth to intimacy and understanding. Unhealthy conflict creates bitterness and resentment. Two major red flags of unhealthy conflict management are stonewalling (the silent treatment) and any form of violence. If someone is a little too angry as a boyfriend/girlfriend, they will be much too angry as a spouse. Marriage typically increases conflict and the potential for anger. What makes you angry?

How do you handle your frustration or anger?

Who should bring up an issue that is bothersome?

What if we disagree both about what should be done and whether it is serious?

Will we go to bed angry at each other?

What is our view of getting help from friends or counselors?

Does he/she share your faith?

The deeper you hold your faith, the more difficult it is to compromise on this, particularly if you decide to have children. A common faith holds a family together, not just on a weekly basis, but on major holidays throughout the year—which means that every such occasion will remind you of your disconnect as a couple if you share a significantly different expression of faith that makes you want to be in two different houses of worship at any one time.

Will they kiss divorce good-bye?

Every marriage eventually proves to be difficult at times. Human nature is such that if there's an easy "off-ramp," we tend to want to take it. Marry someone who is committed to working through every challenge you face without considering divorce as an option.

Will they be a spectacular parent?

You're not just choosing your future husband or wife; you're choosing your children's future dad or mom. It's impossible for you to imagine how much you'll love your children; they will pull emotions out of you that you didn't even know you had. And on the day you bring them home, you'll be so glad you picked someone who will be a fantastic parent, or you'll grieve that they have to put up with someone who is neglectful or, even worse, abusive. If you plan on having children, your marriage isn't just about you. Your future spouse's suitability as a parent is a major deal to consider.

Do they pray?

The older we get, the more it seems we need to pray. Our circle of influence widens. People ask us to pray for them. The task of being married requires daily prayer—we pray about how to love each other, for the strength to serve unselfishly, and for wisdom for many decisions. Being married to an active pray-er is a true blessing. By the way, a quick test to know how often someone prays is simply listening to what they talk about. Do they ever share what God is challenging them with? If they're not regularly talking about God, they're not regularly talking to God. If he/she never shares anything about their devotional times, that's a good sign that they don't really have significant devotional times.

Do they know how to forgive?
James 3:2 says, "We all stumble in many ways." That includes you. The Bible testifies that, in marriage (and out), you will stumble in many ways. If you marry someone who doesn't know how to forgive, your marriage will soon be weighted down with heavy resentment and bitterness.

Do they know how to communicate?
Communication is essential to build new intimacy when infatuation fades (which it will). If you marry someone who is fearful of communication or unskilled at communication, your marriage will fall into an intimacy rut. You can't love what you don't know. You can't be truly loved if you're not truly known. And the only way to know and be known by another person is to communicate—openly, honestly, sincerely, humbly. Women, however much your boyfriend talks to you, imagine marriage will have 25% less talk. (I'm not suggesting it should be that way, just that it often is.) Will that be enough? If he's already borderline in this area, you're likely to become very frustrated after marriage.

Is he/she humble?
The only thing worse than being married to someone who isn't perfect, is being married to someone who isn't perfect but who thinks they are. People without humility can never grow; they spend all their energy defending themselves rather than evaluating themselves and making appropriate corrections. Ask yourself, does this person ever serve others, or do they insist on being served? Do they show empathy toward the feelings of others or are they always trying to impress? Do they show initiative in caring for others, or are they obsessed with how they are treated or appreciated?

Are they a giver or a taker?

The sad reality is, some people are givers and some people are takers. Givers don't always mind being in a relationship with a taker because they like to give; it brings them joy. But marriage is a long journey and there will eventually be seasons when the giver needs to receive. In those instances, can your taker learn to give? In most cases, sadly, the answer is no. When a taker has to give, he feels sorry for himself even more than he feels empathy for you. Ask yourself, when you spend time with your partner, do you feel drained or invigorated? Would you describe the relationship as healing and supportive, or exhausting and combative?

What does their "fruit" look like?

Talking about "character" can sound so general that it isn't helpful. A famous Bible passage breaks this down into two lists of "fruit." One is desirable, one isn't. Go through these lists and see which one most accurately describes the person you're considering marrying: **The "Watch Out" List:** *Sexual irresponsibility; Impurity and debauchery (is this person drawn to the crude?); Hatred, discord, and jealousy; Fits of rage; Selfishness; Divisive and envious; Drunkenness.* **The "Go" List**: *Love; Joy; Peace; Patience; Kindness; Goodness; Faithfulness; Gentleness; Self-control.*

When you consider marriage with someone, ask yourself, DOES THIS PERSON BRING OUT THE BEST IN ME? This question may sound trivial, but its answer will reveal much about the future quality of your relationship. As we have seen throughout this book, God's purpose for dating and marriage is that two people share sacrificial love. For that reason, you want to find someone who is passionate about investing in your life and vice versa.

In healthy relationships, people help each other to flourish. I call this **"relational cheerleading."** I don't mean positive pep talks. Rather, relational cheerleading is creating an encouraging environment in which another person can safely try new experiences and grow as an individual. This type of supportive atmosphere fosters intimacy. You go beyond telling someone, **"You can do it"** and involve yourself in his or her accomplishments.

In the same way, I encourage you to honestly assess what kind of influence your courtship partner has upon your life. Does he or she truly care about your growth and maturity? Does he or she encourage you to meet new people, try new hobbies, and maintain your faith in God? Does he or she have a history of sacrificing time, money, or attention to support you physically and spiritually? Or does he or she simply use you for his or her happiness?

Many singles have been demoralized by courting an immature person. Courting someone who is selfish shuts down a person's desire to grow spiritually, expand his or her interests, or get involved with others. Instead, Christ wants singles to spur each other on to grow in love and maturity.

You can start this process by asking your courtship partner about his or her dreams and goals. What has he or she always wanted to do? In what area could he or she use your support? Determine how you might reasonably help your date achieve his or her desire. Then court each other long enough so that an extended pattern of supportive behavior can emerge. Remember that courting is a prelude to marriage, and marriage is a commitment to an imperfect person for his or her highest good. Marrying someone who is committed to helping you flourish is a delight. On the other hand, living alone is better than marrying someone who does not deeply care about you.

How to Ask Questions Regarding Someone's Past:

Which childhood experiences influence your behavior and attitude the most?

Could any feelings of affection and romance be revived if you met a previous boyfriend/girlfriend even though you feel strongly committed to me?

Is there anything in your past I should be aware of?

What did you dislike the most about your previous partners?

If your past boyfriends/girlfriends listed your most negative characteristics, what would they be?

Do you keep letters and memorabilia from past relationships? Why or why not?

Are you comfortable continuing this relationship if there are things in my past that I am not willing to share with you?

Have you ever been involved in any criminal activities? What were they?

Did your mother or father abuse each other or you in any way- sexually, emotionally, or physically?

Have you ever been able to overcome a bad habit? What was it? Have you ever been violent in past relationships?

How to ask Sexual Questions in a Courtship

I think sex is/will be?

I think a healthy marriage involves sex [ ] per week or [ ] per month.

Real sex in marriage differs from Hollywood in the following ways...

I think being naked in front of someone is?

On a scale from one to ten, sex is a [ ] in importance in a good marriage.

What sex means to me is?

Talking about sex feels?

Being spontaneous or creative in marriage sex sounds?

If we eliminated physical attraction from our relationship, what would be left?

What is the best way for me to show that I love you?

If I put on weight, will it affect our sexual relationship? How?

Is it important for you to know that I'm a virgin? Why or why not?

What do I do that causes you to question my love?

What turns you off sexually?

How would our relationship be affected if for medical reasons we could not have children?

Do you think being in love means:

(1) Never having to say you're sorry,
(2) Always having to say you're sorry,
(3) Knowing when to say you're sorry, or
(4) Being the first to say I'm sorry?

I feel loved when?

The way I show love to people is?

Which of the following are ways I feel most loved?
Time spent with,
Words of encouragement/
Praise,
Gifts,
Being touched and hugged in a non-sexual manner,
When people do things for (serve) me.

Showing affection in front of kids or friends is?

Intimacy is developed through?

I think a good marriage needs at least [ ] hours a day (or week) of focused communication to stay connected.

Can I trust Him / Her, with Me?

Have there been times when you were uncomfortable with the way I behaved with the opposite sex? If so, when and what did I do?

What do I do now or what could I do in the future that would make you mistrust me?

Would you be comfortable transferring all your money into my bank account?

Who comes first, your spouse or your children?

Is trust automatic until something occurs that takes it away, or does it evolve over time?

Do you trust me with money?

Is it permissible for us to open each other's mail?

Miscellaneous Discussion Starters

What is your attitude toward pets? Indoor? Outdoor?

What are your political leanings?

What is your general attitude toward civil government?

What is (are) your favorite sources for news?

What are your interests, hobbies, talents?

What are your income producing (vocational) skills?

What is your attitude toward family (home) business?

What do you value most highly in life? What next?

What do you tend to do in your spare time?

What is your involvement in sports? Do you participate, attend games, watch it on TV? To what extent? What sports do you like?

What are your thoughts on alternative medicine?

What are your thoughts on immunizations?

Do you prefer to live in the city, suburbs, town, or country; farm, seaside, mountains, or desert? Why?

Describe a typical week day in your life from start to finish.

Describe a typical Saturday in your life from start to finish.

What will we do for fun weekly (e.g. go to the movies)? Will we vacation annually (or more or less frequently)? I think my wife's number one complaint is that I love being home, I can stay home all day and be perfectly content. While she's on the opposite end of that spectrum. What's my point? It will be mutually beneficial to come to some common grounds on your activities and vacations in advance.

Are you closer to your mother or father? Why?

Do you prefer a set daily work schedule or flexible work activities and timetables?

What do you fear?

What influence, if any, do you believe my family should have on our relationship?

What are your views on pornography?
How would you react if our son or daughter told us they were gay?
Do you harbor any racial prejudice?
How do you feel about having guns in our home?
Is there anyone close to you who feels we should not get married?
Why? Should we this?
What health problems do you have?
Have you ever had any psychological problems?
When you are in a bad mood, how should I deal with it?
Do you like pets?

Other Things That Must Be Considered Before Getting Married

Do you have any bad habits (e.g. Gambling, Shopping, Eating, Drinking, Sex, etc.)? A must ask question. You want to know if your partner has any bad habits that will affect your relationship. Most people have at least one bad habit. A single bad habit, if not attended to, can unravel an entire relationship. If you don't ask, your partner may not tell.

The following are thirty questions that can help you achieve more clarity about your relationship—what's working, what's not, and why. Please keep in mind there are no wrong or right answers, just *insightful* ones:

Do you completely trust each other?

Do you believe in soul mates, and if so, do you believe you are each other's?

When was the last time you said, "I love you?" If it's been a while, why?

Are you satisfied with the intimacy you share?

How often do you laugh together?

Do you feel you have made personal sacrifices for your relationship, and have they been reciprocated?

When you think of your partner, do you smile?

Do you feel threatened when others find your partner attractive, and why?

Do you believe your partner is your biggest advocate?

How do you feel about your partner's views on finances?

Do you enjoy spending time with your partner's relatives? Friends?

Do either of you dredge up resentments in arguments, and why have you struggled to let them go?

How do you feel when your partner arrives home after being away?

Is your partner your best friend?

Is there a secret you are keeping that if your partner knew, you feel you would lose them?

Do you feel that your partner accepts you?

When did you realize you had fallen in love, and how do you feel when you think about it?

Have you seen each other at your best and worst?

Would you ever consider having an affair? Why? Why not?

Are you excited about your future together?

Do you feel your relationship is a true partnership?

When was your last romantic outing?

Does it bother you if your partner has friends of the opposite sex, and why?

Do you accept each other's belief systems?

When was the last time you talked about your future together, and were you on the same page?

Do you feel as if you can communicate without saying a word?

What is your happiest memory of your time together? Your worst? Are there more happy memories than unhappy ones?

What is a relationship deal breaker for you, and have you overlooked one in this relationship?

How do you feel about the last, in-depth conversation you and your partner had?

Do you show your love for each other often, and if not, why?

If you are seeking clarity about your relationship, the best source of insight is from within. You just need to be unafraid to ask for the answers you seek. Then trust those answers and yourself.

Whether you are the jealous partner or whether your spouse is the jealous one, irrational jealousy can eventually destroy your marriage. Here are answers to frequent questions about jealousy and things you can do to overcome jealousy in your marriage.

What is Jealousy?

A. "Jealousy is a reaction to a perceived threat -- real or imagined -- to a valued relationship or to its quality. A nationwide survey of marriage counselors indicates that jealousy is a problem in one third of all couples coming for marital therapy."

A little jealousy is reassuring and may even be programmed into us. It's very common. A lot of jealousy is scary, and has driven people to some very dangerous behavior. There's no reason to believe that jealousy will improve with time or marriage... Because jealousy goes right to the core of the self and its roots are deep, it is not something that can be banished by wishful thinking.

9 Steps To Drama Free Friendships - Is Jealousy Natural?
A.   In relationships where feelings of jealousy are mild and occasional, it reminds the couple not to take each other for granted. It can encourage couples to appreciate each other and make a conscious effort to make sure the other person feels valued ... Jealousy heightens emotions, making **love** feel stronger and sex more passionate. In small, manageable doses, jealousy can be a positive force in a relationship. But when it's intense or irrational, the story is very different ... Occasional jealousy is natural and can keep a relationship alive, but when it becomes intense or irrational it can seriously damage a relationship.

What Do Jealous People Feel?

A. Jealous individuals experience a multitude of feelings including fear, anger, humiliation, sense of failure, feeling suspicious, threatened, rage, grief, worry, envy, sadness, doubt, pain, and self-pity. Jealousy keeps us under a sense of discouraging frustration and disappointment. It makes us gloomy. It is such a depressing feeling that we cannot tell about it to even our best friends nor can we contain it within ourselves. Consequently, it leaves us with an inconvenience of a peculiar misery and if allowed to grow unchecked beyond a limit, it works like a slow poison to our healthy nature.

Why are People Jealous?

A. Jealousy can be caused by many factors.

Unrealistic expectations about marriage in general. Unrealistic expectations about your relationship with your spouse. A misguided sense of ownership of your spouse. Hurtful experience of abandonment in the past.

Poor self-image. Insecurity. Fear of being abandoned or betrayed. Fear of losing someone or something important to them.

Intense possessiveness. A desire to control.

What are the Consequences of Irrational Jealousy in Marriage?

A. "For those who experience abnormal jealousy, the emotion sets up a self-fulfilling prophecy. As their associates try to avoid them, their worst fears of losing love and respect are realized.
Some of the underlying or reactive feelings of jealousy may also be:

Resentment.

Increased **lack of trust**.

Anger.

Defensiveness.

More arguments.

Need for continual reassurance.

Depression.

Desire for revenge.

Constant questioning.

Physical reactions such as trembling, feeling dizzy, change in sleep patterns, and a change in eating habits.

End of your marriage.

"People who feel secure and like themselves tend to be less jealous of others and less possessive of their partners, while those who have experienced abandonment or betrayal in their lives can become overwhelmed with jealousy ... If you feel jealous, or if your partner does, it doesn't matter. Eventually, jealousy will erode your relationship and destroy your marriage ... Jealousy is a way to exert control in a relationship ... Getting control of your jealousy does not mean getting control of your partner, it means getting a handle on your own emotions."

How Can a Couple Handle Jealousy?

A.   "Can jealousy be overcome? The answer is yes, but with great effort. Like most other difficult emotional experiences, jealousy, if treated correctly, can be a trigger for growth. It can become the first step in increased self-awareness and greater understanding both of your mate and of the relationship.

How to recognize where jealousy comes from and how to cope with it"

Admit your jealous behavior and accept that your jealousy is hurting your marriage.

Discuss the roots of your or your spouse's jealous feelings.

Don't spy on your spouse.

As a jealous spouse, make a decision to change your behavior. You may need to get individual counseling.

Realize you can't control someone else.

Together, set fair ground rules that you can both live with.

If you are the non-jealous partner, don't lie or try to hide where you are or what you are doing.

Seek professional help as a couple if necessary.

What every Man is Expected to Lead His Home

Is Courtship Leadership Properly Established in Your Relationship?

When you are courting, you always have the option to leave if someone acts unreasonably. In marriage, though, you make a lifelong commitment. Therefore, selecting wisely is imperative, especially when it comes to the issue of leadership. The leader generally determines the maturity level of a relationship, and the best way to discern how someone handles leadership is to observe him or her in courting. The individual who leads during courting usually will lead in marriage. Unfortunately, many singles wrestle with relational leadership for two reasons: Either they misunderstand how someone becomes a leader or they misinterpret the leader's true purpose.

Our culture suggests that anyone who wants to lead must exhibit superior performance to earn the title. If a leader makes too many bad decisions, he or she can be fired and replaced. This definition, however, is not how God determines the leader of a marriage relationship.

But I want you to understand that Christ is the head of every man, and the man is the head of a woman, and God is the head of Christ.... For man does not originate from woman, but woman from man; for indeed man was not created for the woman's sake, but woman for the man's sake. However, in the Lord, neither is woman independent of man, nor is man independent of woman. For as the woman originates from the man, so also the man has his birth through the woman; and all things originate from God (1 Corinthians 11:3,8-12).

For the husband is the head of the wife, as Christ also is the head of the church, He Himself being the Savior of the body. But as the church is subject to Christ, so also the wives ought to be to their husbands in everything. Husbands, love your wives, just as Christ also loved the church and gave Himself up for her (Ephesians 5:23-25).

These verses clearly explain how God established the leadership structure for husbands and wives in marriage. His hierarchy reaches beyond the roles of men and women. Consider the following points:

1. God is the Head of Christ.

2. Christ is the Head of every man and woman.

3. A husband is the head of his wife.

4. A woman is subject to her husband.

5. A husband is to love his wife sacrificially, just as Christ loves the church.

6. Men and women are not independent of each other.

How do you know whether the person you date accepts God's leadership structure? Observe his or her willingness to lead or submit. You may be dating an immature person. When someone is unwilling to try out his or her relational role in courting, he or she will unlikely embrace it in marriage. Passive or dominating behavior boils down to a lack of faith in the authority of God.

Besides equating leadership with performance, some singles do not understand what leadership truly involves. God's definition of a leader is not simply "decision maker." A real leader sacrifices his desires for the benefit of his wife. God says that the man's job is to love his wife just as Christ loved the church. In the same manner, God urges men to love their wives sacrificially. Her needs and concerns are supposed to become his focus. In addition, his role includes maintaining an environment of intimacy. This means accepting her, forgiving her, protecting her, and considering her interests as more important than his. When a husband loves his wife sacrificially, he creates a physical illustration of Christ's love for believers. Therefore, ladies, observe whether the man you date behaves in this way. Does he know what is important to you? Does he sacrifice his interests for yours? Is he willing to disagree with you when he believes it is for your benefit?

After The Decision to Get Married Has Happened

Planning a wedding is wonderful, beautiful, stressful, and sometimes just plain crazy. There are so many details to plan and then accomplish before the day rolls around! Where do you start? You've got to take care of invitations, flowers, catering, cakes, clothes, the ceremony, the honeymoon and so much more! It's pretty obvious why most couples give themselves months (and sometimes years) between saying "I will" and "I do."

What month do we want to get married in?

Who should be invited to the wedding?

What colors are we going to use?

What kind of food do we want to serve?

Do you want children?

If we are unable to have children, should we adopt?

Do you anticipate raising our children
(1) the same way you were raised
(2) completely differently from the way you were raised
(3) a mixture of both?

How long would you like to wait before having children?

Other than formal schooling, what types of education will our children get and how will they receive them?

When we have children, who will change the diapers, heat the bottles, prepare the meals, do the housework, bathe the child, get up in the middle of the night when a child is crying, take the child to the doctor, buy clothing, and dress the child?

What types of discipline would you implement to correct a child's or a teenager's behavior? Were these practices you experiences or are they new ones you have developed on your own?

What does commitment mean to me? Do I have a role model to follow who helps me see how to navigate through the tough times?

What changes do I expect to see after the wedding?

What are the common goals and dreams we want to achieve?

Where will we live?

How many children do we want?

Who will clean the toilet and take out the trash?

What color will the bedroom be?

Where will we spend the holidays?

How will we continue to educate ourselves on being happily married? You want to discuss the spiritual needs of the relationship, and you also want to discuss the growth needs, as it relates to self-development and the development of your marriage. You want to have plans to grow together, or you will grow apart. Remember, failing to plan, is planning to fail.
What kind of marriage do I want?

How happy am I in this relationship?

Who is responsible for my happiness?

How much fun do we have on our dates?

Do I have fond memories of our courtship?

How often will we have sex? You want to find out now if you're going to be having sex every day or once a month. That's all I'll say about that.

How are we different? Could this be a source of future conflict? Do our differences complement each other?

Do you anticipate maintaining your single lifestyle after we are married? That is, will you spend just as much time with your friends, family and work colleagues? Why or why not?

How did your family resolve conflicts when you were growing up? Do you approve or disapprove of that method? What will you change or not change to resolve conflicts in your future family?

Is there anything about marriage that frightens you?

If I wanted to move away from our families for work, would you support me?

How would it affect you if I travel on my own frequently to
(1) visit family,
(2) earn income,
(3) pursue a hobby, or
(4) deal with stress?

Suppose we are experiencing trouble in our marriage. In what order will you seek help from the following to resolve our conflicts:
(1) divorce lawyer,
(2) your parents,
(3) a brother or sister
(4) a marriage counselor,
(5) me,
(6) a church leader? Why?

How will you support my hobbies?

How do you feel about having our parents come to live with us if the need arises?

Is there anything you would regret not being able to do or accomplish if you married me?

How will we schedule holidays with our families?

The list goes on with details that will help make this day a very special memory for years to come.

Top Marriage Mistakes

There is often a pattern to the marital problems and issues that people tend to have. You definitely do not want these problems and if you do, think about coming together to make some changes. Here's a list of the top ten things that you need to try to avoid, or fix, in your own **marriage**.

Lack of Respect:
Showing a lack of respect to your partner is quite troubling in a marriage. Don't badmouth your spouse to your friends or associates. Spouses need to be thanked. They need to know they are appreciated. You both should be speaking kindly to each other.

Not Listening to Your Spouse:
You should not simply hear the words spoken, but show you are actively engaged in conversation as well. This includes allowing your mind to wander, paying more attention to the computer or television set, ignoring body language, and interrupting. Expecting your spouse to be a mind reader is another big communication mistake.

Little or No Physical Intimacy
A lack of physical affection or sexual intimacy will turn lovers into roommates. This is a death knell for a marriage. Seek medical advise and therapeutic counseling if necessary. Spouses should not leave their partners wondering why there is no interest in sex. It's not fair to either of you.

Always Having to Be Right
It is impossible for you to be always right. If you try, you may win the battle, but lose the war! Having to be right includes lecturing your mate, or having to have the last word. Very few people can love a know-it-all forever. Admit when you make a mistake or that you don't have all the answers. And please, please, don't answer

every simple question your spouse asks with a long-winded boring dissertation on the topic. That doesn't answer the question.

Not Walking the Talk
Actions do speak louder than words. When you say you'll do something, do it. When you say you won't do something, follow through. Keep your promises. If this does not happen, it will erode at the trust and safety between you. Your partner MUST be able to count on you!

Hurtful Teasing
If your spouse says the teasing is hurtful, considers it a put down, or thinks that it is inappropriate, then stop it. Claiming that your spouse doesn't have a sense of humor or is too sensitive is being inconsiderate and unkind.

Dishonesty
There is no room in a marriage for deceit or dishonesty. Having lies and secrets in your relationship can create distance and lack of trust between the two of you. Be honest with each other. Honesty is considered a must-have by most married couples.

Nasty Habits Can Hurt Your Marriage
Bad habits like having gross personal hygiene habits, always being late, or nitpicking everything are not good for your relationship. The worst part is when you know you are annoying and you continue to annoy. If your spouse brings up an issue he or she finds aggravating, make a concerted effort to make a change.

Being Selfish or Greedy
Being selfish is when you spend money on yourself, but make a big deal if your spouse spends a dime. It's not wanting to open your home to friends and family because you prefer to be alone and don't want the hassle of entertaining. It's hogging the remote, only going to cheap restaurants when you could afford better, or not

watching movies your spouse wants to see. It's also, being uncompromising.

Having Temper Tantrums
Every couple needs to be able to handle conflict in a constructive way. Having an angry outburst so that you can win an argument will make you the loser in the end. It's also manipulative. Learn how to fight fair and to make your marital relationship the winner of any disagreement the two of you have. If you still find anger get's the best of you, get some professional help or read a self-help book on the topic.